Developing a Curriculum Model for Civically Engaged Art Education

This volume explores art as a means of engendering youth civic engagement and draws on research conducted with young people in the United States to develop a unique curriculum model for civically engaged art education (CEAE).

Combining concepts from civics and arts education, chapters posit that artistic thinking, making, and acting form the basis for creative research into social and political issues which affect young people and are key to promoting civic participation. Focusing on critical, creative, and dynamic forms of youth cultural production inspired by local people, places, and events, the text demonstrates how educators' curricular choices can engage students in researching social movements and arts-based activism. The authors draw from well-established areas such as arts-based research, civic engagement, and maker-centered learning to present their educational model through illustrative examples.

Offering a timely consideration of the relationship between art education and civic education, this book will appeal to scholars and students of the sociology of education, as well as arts and teacher research, and pre-service teacher education.

Sara Scott Shields is an Associate Professor of Art Education at Florida State University, USA.

Rachel Fendler is an Associate Professor of Art Education at Florida State University, USA.

Routledge Research in Arts Education

Books in the series include:

Addressing Issues of Mental Health in Schools through the Arts
Teachers and Music Therapists Working Together
Edited by Jane Tarr and Nick Clough

Educating for Peace through Theatrical Arts
International Perspectives on Peacebuilding Instruction
Edited by Candice C. Carter and Rodrigo Benza Guerra

Artist-Teacher Practice and the Expectation of an Aesthetic Life
Creative Being in the Neoliberal Classroom
Carol Wild

Counternarratives from Asian American Art Educators
Identities, Pedagogies, and Practice beyond the Western Paradigm
Edited by Ryan Shin, Maria Lim, Oksun Lee, and Sandrine Han

Children are Artists: Supporting Children's Learning Identity as Artists
Penny Hay

Developing a Curriculum Model for Civically Engaged Art Education
Engaging Youth through Artistic Research
Sara Scott Shields and Rachel Fendler

Developing a Curriculum Model for Civically Engaged Art Education

Engaging Youth through Artistic Research

Sara Scott Shields and Rachel Fendler

Routledge
Taylor & Francis Group

NEW YORK AND LONDON

First published 2024
by Routledge
605 Third Avenue, New York, NY 10158

and by Routledge
4 Park Square, Milton Park, Abingdon, Oxon, OX14 4RN

Routledge is an imprint of the Taylor & Francis Group, an informa business

ISBN: 978-1-032-05778-1 (hbk)
ISBN: 978-1-032-05811-5 (pbk)
ISBN: 978-1-003-19910-6 (ebk)

DOI: 10.4324/9781003199106

Typeset in Sabon
by KnowledgeWorks Global Ltd.

This book is dedicated to the students who participated in this project. We are forever grateful for the vulnerability, curiosity, and bravery you showed as we dove into the Foot Soldiers program. Your personalities, processes, and artworks forever changed the way we understand art education and gave us a vision of the kind of people to whom we wish to entrust our future. This is a future for not just us but our children, who were all born during the four years we worked on this project. This book is also dedicated to them. Adalaide, Teo, William, and Ivet, the possibility of your futures has driven us to keep searching for ways to make the world a better place.

Contents

Figures, table, and box

Figures

Table

Box

Acknowledgments

We want to start by thanking our partners:

To Tim, thank you for always offering to pick up the kids, for covering the late nights, and for pushing me to make time for this work. When we met, I told you that if this relationship was going to work you would just have to be willing to follow me, and instead of following me, you have walked beside me. I love you!

(Sara)

To Roger, I am grateful everyday for the reminder that there are, in fact, things more important than work. When research and the lives of students feel like they require so much of my attention, it is an inexplicable pleasure to receive from you a wealth of care and support that puts everything else into perspective. Thank you for everything.
(Rachel)

We want to also acknowledge teachers in states like Florida, who continue to show up and do the hopeful work of building a future for public education. We are inspired by your bravery and dedication to a better tomorrow.

We were exceptionally lucky to have collaborated with several graduate and undergraduate research assistants, who made the implementation of this project possible.

Danielle Henn, a doctoral candidate, was a pivotal collaborator throughout the project. Danielle collaborated closely with us on the design of the field guides and was an instructor during both years of the program. Thank you, Danielle, for the late nights, the beautiful demo projects you made during your excursions into the city, your thoughtful and generative role as an instructor, and for sticking with us, Braxton Hicks and all.

Lydia Moss, as an undergraduate research assistant from Theater, was with us for the inception of the project. Thank you Lydia for your energy, your engaging way with the students, and your knowledge of Tallahassee.

Brie Medina, a master's student and pre-service teacher, joined us in our second year. Brie tirelessly built a repository of case files for this project, turning our research into a resource guide that is now available to teachers. She also assisted with updating and improving the field guides and served as instructor in our second year. Thank you Brie for your collaboration, insight, dry humor, and rigor.

Program documentation was an essential component of the project, and it is thanks to two collaborators that we were able to share the work in this book. Victoria Munsell, in 2018, and Sarah Johns, in 2019, captured our process through close and creative observation. Thanks to you both for allowing us to hold on so closely to this experience.

We also want to thank the city of Tallahassee and all the institutions and individuals who gave their time and resources to our project: first, the Meek-Eaton Black Archives and Museum, for maintaining such an inspiring and comprehensive collection of Black history; also the State Library and Archives of Florida, specifically Joshua Goodman, who made an extensive collection of resources related to the civil rights movement in Tallahassee available to the students in this project.

We want to extend a debt of gratitude to the tireless individuals who participated in the civil rights movement here in Tallahassee. In particular we want to thank Gloria Anderson, Daryl Scott, Annie Harris, Bernice Daniels Presley, and Henry Steele for sharing their first-hand accounts with the students in the Foot Soldiers program. Your stories still echo in our souls and continue to inspire us to learn more about this city we all call home.

We would like to thank the local artists who took time out of their schedules to come and talk to the students in the program. Cosby Hayes, Sarah Painter, and Adreenah Wynn, your creativity reverberated in the work the students engaged in, keep making the world a more beautiful place.

Finally, this project was made possible by generous funding provided by Florida State University through the Arts & Humanities Program Enhancement Grant and the Committee on Faculty Research Support program.

Introduction
Civics, Art, and Education

The American political landscape is marked by a historic partisan animosity, with alarming and increasing instances of gerrymandering, voter suppression laws, and broad censorship of topics related to injustice in the school curriculum. Since 2018, when our research for this book began, we have borne witness to the ways in which school board meetings, library collections, and syllabi have made national headlines, putting schools, once again, in the spotlight of the political and cultural tides of a divided and fractured civic sphere in the United States. This situation begs the essential question: what should we do? This question is offered by the National Academy of Education (Lee et al., 2021) as one that defines civic reasoning. It is a question that requires the inquirer to identify a civic community (who is "we"?), review avenues for response (what can be done?), and make a reasoned decision for action (what should be done?). Developing an answer to this question is the project of civic engagement. Hence, we begin this volume by posing the question to ourselves. What should educators do about the democratic crisis facing our students, one that is apparent in our communities and impacting our classrooms? In the face of a difficult situation, this volume considers hope. After all, what is civic behavior if not a commitment to a better possible future? Taking seriously the need to bolster civic competencies, we will explore how art education helps young people build an understanding of themselves as civic actors. Our aim is to reveal art education as a potential site for delivering a creative and rich civics curriculum that complements traditional civics instruction in other disciplinary areas and increases exposure to civic instruction in schools. In today's civic environment, hope is needed. What should we, educators, do? One hopeful possibility is the realm of curriculum development, where we can work to create experiences for students to grapple with and become part of the civic fabric of their communities. But before we can do the work of developing curriculum together, we feel it is important for you to know how we came together as a team. What follows is a brief introduction to who we are, where we come from, where we are now, and who we think this curriculum work should be for.

Rachel

I arrived in Tallahassee, Florida after accepting the position of Assistant Professor of Art Education, my first faculty job after completing graduate school. I was drawn into the field of art education from a background in visual studies that evolved into a curiosity about the informal and creative learning practices that shape young people's lives. A particular interest I had was in the expansive and unpredictable nature of learning, and the ways in which young people's interests and desires could pull them into trajectories that could both support but also resist formal curriculum. As a result, I had begun to study how the learning process took students somewhere, creating social spaces, introducing new places, and giving rise to new contexts within which young people could explore modes of being in the world. My journey in graduate school unfolded in Barcelona, Spain, a city whose complicated history situates the politics of memory, history, preservation, and civic participation as central concerns in the cultural sector.

Once in Tallahassee, I established a collaboration with a municipal recreation center for teens, where I began a weekly videolab for interested participants. Through this collaboration with a small group of teenagers we began to explore the teen center, then a city block, and as interests and resources grew, we took the project out into different neighborhoods. At the same time, through my work in a preservice art education program, I was becoming increasingly invested in how to support the development of formal curriculum and the challenges facing public teachers. Both within the university and outside of it, the project engaging young people in a creative exploration of the city became more intentional. I began to consider how the city could serve as a curriculum, and how a curriculum could help activate meaningful learning experiences for students. It is at this moment when my formal collaboration with Sara began.

Sara

I come from a long line of educators, my grandmother worked in an elementary school as a teacher aide. After her, all three of her daughters eventually found their way to the world of education. Her oldest daughter, my mother, was a nurse who later became a professor and director of a nursing PhD program. My father taught agriculture at both a community college and a high school. When I left home to go to college I received a teaching fellowship, giving me four years of education in exchange for four years of service to the state. While teaching has always seemed to be my destination, the arts have been my destiny. I love making art, looking at art, and filling my home with art. I think in pictures and dream in vivid color. So when I took the fellowship for teaching, I thought I was leaving behind my love of art. I'm not sure why teaching art didn't occur to me immediately, but the irony doesn't escape me as I now work as a pre-service art educator. I eventually settled into a ceramics BFA program and begrudgingly fulfilled my obligation to become a licensed teacher. I graduated in December and took the first job I was offered. I packed my bags and moved to the coast of NC to teach art at a Title I School. I was hired to teach Art I, Art II, and Ceramics. I worked there for seven years. It was one of the best times of my life. Never quite able to stop learning, I continued forward, pursuing a master's degree and eventually resigning from my position to begin a doctoral program.

In my doctoral program, I returned to what I knew about art classrooms, that students wanted to make things, they wanted to be given freedom, they wanted to do something meaningful. I spent time thinking back on my experience in the classroom, remembering how much student investment changed when I shifted the locus of control away from me and to the students, how the outcomes of projects looked better when I didn't dictate the content of student work. So, I studied this in my doctoral program, looking closely at how students used self-guided sketchbooks or visual journals to develop relationships with course content. I graduated with a PhD and again, took the first job I was offered. I came to Florida State University's Art Education program with big plans for studying how artmaking allows young people to access deep, introspective understandings, how the process of making is more important than the products the teacher sent home, and how thinking like an artist opens up possibilities for teaching and learning in art classrooms. And while I still believe these things to be true, Rachel's arrival in Tallahassee, just a year after mine, has pushed me to think more carefully about what we (art educators) are doing to impact our world.

Sara and Rachel in collaboration

As new faculty at an R1 university, we decided that to be successful we would need to find ways to support each other. While our research was happening in separate spheres, we began attending conferences together. As an act of support, we often found ourselves attending each other's presentations. The more we listened to the work the other was doing, the more we started to realize that perhaps our work wasn't so different. As our working relationship grew, so did our friendship. In these early days, we spent time talking about anything from how young academics had the time to start families, to the best ways to design curriculum for our classes, to formulating sustainable research agendas. Somewhere in these conversations, our long-term goals merged, and we found ourselves beginning to explore how we might bring our different skills and expertise together to form a collaborative research agenda.

We have now been working together for about five years. Over these last five years, we have worked with the curricular themes of local history and memory through a range of projects that have used art to ground student and teacher explorations of civic engagement. We have sought out ways to have young people engage their communities while also making evocative, exceptional artwork. Early iterations of this project were situated in afterschool programs where we worked with teens to explore the city of Tallahassee. In these collaborations, we invited young people to get to know Tallahassee by walking, talking, and filming a historically Black neighborhood. This experience shaped much of our interest in how the arts invited investigation and participation in the local community. During our weekly trips, we witnessed young people meet neighbors and learn about community histories. We were invited into people's homes to collect oral histories, and it was in backyards and living rooms that these conversations opened up dialogue (Fendler & Shields, 2018). Spending time in the community with teens initiated our own exploration into the rich history of our city, Tallahassee, Florida.

Discovering Tallahassee

There is a memorial in Tallahassee that captures the ethos of our project. The Smokey Hollow memorial consists of three "spirit houses," a series of metal structures whose beams echo the shape of the shotgun houses that populated a neighborhood that has long since disappeared. Smokey Hollow was a vibrant Black community that was targeted by municipal rezoning measures in the 1950s, pushing Black businesses and homes away from the downtown area. The spirit houses are made only of beams bearing inscriptions of quotations from past inhabitants. Informational panels on their doorsteps share maps, archival images, and oral histories. On the floor of one spirit house, visitors can see the layout of how furniture would have sat within these walls. The site holds space for a rich history that honors the past but it is not triumphant. The memorial is stark and evocative, it appears to be as much a commentary on memory itself as it is about the site it remembers. This memorial encapsulated, for us, the depth and complexity of Tallahassee's past, and the ways in which the city invests in remembering it. A powerful teaching tool, the memorial uses art to tell us about historical moments, offers primary sources, such as oral histories and archival images, and imparts an evocative story about the power of communities in developing a sense of shared meaning and belonging within a city. The presence of this memorial invited the questions: What other places in the city hold on to history? How are the arts used to tell these stories?

We had already known, through previous projects, that the city was a powerful curriculum for students, so we set off to formalize an approach to using the city as the basis for an arts program. We began to research other public memorials in the city and discovered the Civil Rights Heritage Walk, a memorial in Tallahassee's downtown area that honors the "foot soldiers" or activists who participated in landmark civil rights protests, such as the bus boycott and lunch counter sit-ins. Over 50 individual foot soldiers are memorialized in bronze footsteps bearing their names. The footsteps are arranged around large terrazzo panels depicting imagery from the Tallahassee civil rights movement. These names catalyzed our research and focused our project on local people, places, and events from the movement.

In the volume that follows, we will share the curriculum that emerged from this research and the way our thinking about art education shifted as a result of teaching this curriculum. As we mapped the civil rights history of our town through its monuments, historical sites, archives, museums, and residents, we gained a sense of our community's living history. At the same time, history continued to unfold around us. During this time, in the aftermath of the shooting at Marjorie Stoneman Douglas High School, student activists were making national headlines. In March of that year, the March for our Lives protest against gun violence in the United States was organized by a coalition of youth organizers. Without time to catch our breath, the following September the world witnessed unprecedented global youth organizing during the Climate Strike. These are not isolated events, as we continue to witness modern-day foot soldiers on the front lines of a struggle for a better life, only this time the foot soldiers are our students.

Envisioning a civically engaged art education

In 2018, we received funding that would support two, week-long summer intensive art programs for upper-middle and high school students. With this funding in place, we designed a week-long experience that positioned students as arts-based researchers by inviting them to explore the legacy of the civil rights movement in Tallahassee. We referred to the project as the Foot Soldier program, in homage to the civil rights activists, or "foot soldiers" commemorated in the Civil Rights Heritage Walk. To prepare, we mapped walking routes, booked tours at archives and museums, sourced archival material, reached out to community members who had been active during the movement, and contacted local artists. Then, we invited students to join us. The results of this program, which took place in 2018 and in 2019, provided the foundation of this book. Together, we cycled through processes of inquiry and discovery, making meaningful connections between the past and present. Students learned about their city and through that process, had the opportunity to see themselves as part of the community as they responded to this experience in their artmaking. The pull into civic life that we witnessed over the course of each week, and how this pull was impacted by and extended into the artmaking process, provided a powerful illustration of how the arts build civic engagement. This volume shares these results in close detail, with the aim of presenting an approach to what we call civically engaged art education.

This book expands on national discussions and initiatives in civic education by intentionally aligning civics with the arts. We intend for this book to reimagine the relationship between civics and art from a curricular perspective, by sharing how these young people used the arts to engage in civic activities. We invite readers of this book to use this volume as a roadmap for incorporating civic objectives into their own art classrooms. The pages will take the reader through curriculum theory, curriculum design, and student outcomes. Section I reviews the theoretical foundations of our project. Here, we look at inputs from research into civic education as well as closely review trends in art education that align with this project. Section II provides a close look at the development of the Foot Soldier program, tracing how we adapted the objectives of civic education for the art classroom. We offer broad curricular strategies, discuss the methods we used in our program, and conclude the section by offering a day-by-day review of how the program was organized. Section III illustrates how students moved through the program. Each chapter has two case studies reviewing students' processes, art pieces, and reflections. This section illustrates how the curriculum led to civic outcomes. Section IV gives a broad review of the civic competencies students demonstrated during the program. In the final chapter, we offer a how-to manual, of sorts, for educators who wish to embark on designing a civically engaged art curriculum. We hope that you find inspiration in these pages to continue this work in your own classroom. Read on for a brief overview of each of the chapters.

Section I: Foundations

Chapter 1: Understanding Civics

Studies on civics and US government courses showed the majority of curricula is focused on democratic processes: the constitution, bill of rights, and voting policies. With this focus on procedures and processes, civics courses rarely involve community-based, local components as part of the curriculum (Shapiro & Brown, 2018). Scholarship in the field of citizenship education has called for reframing the conversation on civics so that it centers on building participatory and justice-oriented citizens (Westheimer & Kahne, 2004). Chapter 1 focuses on how we might understand civic education as something bigger than learning about political participation. We present a vision of civic education that holds equitable access to learning about civic engagement as central, and highlights the importance of young people's personal connection to content. Through this discussion, we draw on the model of cultural citizenship to help us reimagine our definition of civics and draw on the arts, as a form of cultural production, to frame the possibilities for developing a curriculum that could be responsive to this expanded notion of civics.

Chapter 2: Teaching Civics through Art

This chapter explores how the world of art education currently overlaps with discourse around civics, with specific attention to the local and the material. It will discuss how art education may draw on civic education in order to design a curriculum that centers young people, their communities, interests, and artmaking as they explore and expand their notion of what civic participation might look like. To do this, the chapter presents a thematic review of the ways in which the field of art education has approached youth civic engagement, covering genres (EG: socially engaged art), curricular approaches (EG: community-based art education), and research contributions (EG: reporting on the outcomes of art education in support of civic engagement). This chapter includes curriculum literature and research that supports our interest in a civically engaged art curriculum that holds people, places, and events as central points of interest in the exploration of the local community.

Section II: Think

Chapter 3: Positioning Students as Arts-Based Researchers

Building on the concepts in Section I by exploring the role of students in the learning process. This chapter considers the centrality of positioning students as independent researchers and revisits the importance of the arts in helping students develop a research process. The emphasis on students as arts based researchers revisits key ideas from Chapters 1 and 2. The chapter reviews how artmaking, as a process of researching developed through material reflection and material engagement (i.e. learning about people, visiting places, and researching events), opens up possibilities for students to make artwork that interprets and applies their understanding (of history, politics, social issues, etc.) to a contemporary, local context. Through this act of filtering research on larger issues through the lens of the local, students begin to see themselves as actors in their communities. The cycle then begins again, as students address how they might impact their immediate community, make artwork that processes this thinking, and design future action pointing toward progress and change. By positioning teens as arts-based researchers, we adapt a student-centered approach to curriculum, one that asks students to identify and utilize their strengths as they move through a personally relevant learning experience (Shields et al., 2020). This chapter establishes how students are at the core of a civically engaged art curriculum that is organized around the curricular guideposts of think | make | act. These three key components are revisited throughout the volume.

Chapter 4: Envisioning Curriculum

In the summers of 2018 and 2019, the authors offered a week-long intensive art program to upper-middle and high school students focused on studying and reflecting on the legacy of the civil rights movement in Tallahassee, Florida. This program, Tallahassee Foot Soldiers, carried the sub-title Change Makers: Then and Now, indicating our interest in approaching a project on the civil rights movement through the possibilities for youth civic action in the present. The program prioritized student-led research and engagement with primary source material, offering an experience where students spoke with activists and artists (people), explored their city (places), visited archives (events), and synthesized their experience through artmaking. By reviewing art as a research process, this chapter provides a clear description of the ways that material or primary sources—people, places, and events—can become a catalyst for student-driven inquiry into local communities. This chapter takes an in-depth look at the authors' curricular choices when designing a civically engaged art education curriculum. This chapter, in dialogue with Section I, offers a view of what centering people, places, and events looks like in practice. Through this discussion, the chapter broadly introduces the research project and think | make | act curriculum design that the remainder of the book focuses on.

Chapter 5: Curriculum Overview

Chapter 5, while brief, takes the reader through the nuanced details of the summer programs. This chapter is an excellent resource to get a clear idea of how the summer programs progressed, who we arranged visits with, what sites we traveled to, and how we set up the pace of each day. While we do not intend this chapter to provide a replicable curricular program, we do hope that seeing the formatting and flow of the week will provide readers with a touchstone for understanding the student experiences we elaborate on in the illustrative cases presented in Section III.

Section III: Make

Chapter 6: Engaging People

Chapter 6 looks at the role of *people* as a curricular building block for civically engaged art education. Here we share how personal, first-person perspectives engage students in an exploration of history and how the experiences of these historical figures tell an impactful story related to contemporary issues. The first case highlights Iyawa, through a discussion of a series of prints. Her prints were inspired by the tenacity of one participant in the civil rights movement and the unjust death of another. The second case highlights Dwayne's research into a foot soldier who disappeared while registering voters during the height of the civil rights movement. The case closes with a discussion of his prints that trace reporting on deaths of young Black men across the decades. Throughout the chapter, we reflect on the use of portraiture in the arts, elaborating on the relevance of this approach as not only an avenue into historical study, but also as an artistic methodology that renders the artist visible.

Chapter 7: Visiting Places

Echoing the format of Chapter 6, Chapter 7 looks at the role of *place* as a curricular building block for civically engaged art education. The chapter begins with an illustrative case highlighting two students, Theo and Zoe, who responded to the experience of walking and visiting sites throughout the city in different ways. The second illustrative case in this chapter follows Viola, and her response to seeing a topsy-turvy doll during a site visit to a museum. This chapter discusses how the summer program focused on place, taking the reader through our trips to historical locations, monuments, the State Archives, and the Meek-Eaton Black Archives. This chapter looks closely at how the experience of standing in history brought the past to life for students.

Chapter 8: Researching Events

This chapter looks at the role of *events* as a curricular building block for civically engaged art education. The chapter includes two illustrative cases focused on defining moments. This chapter looks closely at how students considered the historical impact of individual actions or collective decisions, through sophisticated interpretations of historic and contemporary events. The first illustrative case looks at Ruby, who wrestled with how historical events impact lived experiences. The second illustrative case follows Hannah, as she created a pen and ink drawing exploring the importance of collective participation, highlighting those who stood in the shadows of leaders. The chapter closes with an exploration of the concept of connection, speculating that students' connection to their community fosters a form of social empathy that can ultimately impact the trajectory of the future.

Section IV: Act

Chapter 9: Imagining Civically Engaged Art Education

In this chapter, we ask the reader to look toward the future of art education. Our hope for art education is that embracing an understanding of civic engagement might allow us to do more to intentionally harness young people's ability to impact society. We believe we must challenge what it means to do interdisciplinary work within our field, by moving away from a model where arts are integrated into other subjects. Instead, we see potential for the art classroom to become a site of deep and meaningful inquiry into local communities by centering young people's inquiry on community histories, stories, and futures. This chapter centers student voices and offers a reflection on how this kind of investigatory artistic practice models a civically engaged approach to learning.

Chapter 10: Designing Curriculum

This chapter offers a pragmatic discussion that begins with a series of essential questions, activities, and curricular development prompts guiding readers as they develop (or teach others to develop) a curriculum that is locally bound, contextually relevant, and socially and politically responsive. Throughout, we underlie the importance of placing the student's lived experience and relationships with their communities at the center of the artistic experience. The chapter challenges readers to use the people, places, and events that shaped their community to design an iteration of the think | make | act curriculum model.

References

Cahill, C., Rios-Moore, I., & Threatts, T. (2008). Different eyes/open eyes: Community-based participatory action research. In J. Cammarota & M. Fine (Eds.), *Revolutionizing education: Youth participatory action research in motion* (pp. 89–124). Routledge.

Clay, K. L., & Rubin, B. C. (2020). "I look deep into this stuff because it's a part of me:" Toward a critically relevant civics education. *Theory & Research in Social Education*, 48(2), 161–181. https://doi.org/10.1080/00933104.2019.1680466

Fendler, R., & Shields, S. S. (2018). Filming Frenchtown: Listening to and learning from storied lives. *LEARNing Landscapes*, 11(2), 141–155. https://doi.org/10.36510/learnland.v11i2.952

Fendler, R., Shields, S. S., & Henn, D. (2020). #thefutureisnow: A model for civically engaged art education. *Art Education*, 73(5), 10–15. https://doi.org/10.1080/00043125.2020.1766922

Lee, C. D., White, G., & Dong, D. (2021). *Educating for civic reasoning and discourse*. National Academy of Education. https://naeducation.org/educating-for-civic-reasoning-and-discourse/

Shapiro, S., & Brown, C. (2018). *The state of civics education*. Center for American Progress. https://www.americanprogress.org/issues/education-k-12/reports/2018/

Shields, S. S., Fendler, R., & Henn, D. (2020). A vision of civically engaged art education: Teens as arts-based researchers. *Studies in Art Education*, 61(2), 123–141. https://doi.org/10.1080/00393541.2020.1740146

Westheimer, J., & Kahne, J. (2004). What kind of citizen? The politics of educating for democracy. *American Educational Research Journal*, 41(2), 237–269. https://doi.org/10.3102/00028312041002237

Section I
Foundations

1 Understanding Civics

Civic participation is essential for a functioning democracy, with signs pointing to a correlation between a decrease in civic engagement among young people and an eroding faith in democracy itself. The Pew Research Center ("Americans' Views of Government," 2022) documented, "since the 2007–2008 financial crisis, no more than about a quarter of Americans have expressed trust in the federal government to do what is right all or most of the time" (p. 10). The lack of trust in government is linked to an erosion of public participation. Using data from the most recent World Values Survey, Foa and Mounk (2016, p. 10., parentheses *added*) reported, "younger generations [in the United States and Europe] are less committed to the importance of democracy, so too are they less likely to be politically engaged." In this context, disengagement from politics is also a disengagement from civic life, "millennials across Western Europe and North America are less engaged than their elders, both in traditional forms of political participation and in oppositional civic activity" (Foa & Mounk, 2016, p. 11). A loss of trust in public institutions stems from and feeds into increased apathy among the public. This paints a stark portrait of the waning commitment of youth to liberal democracy, and points to the vulnerability of a core value of Western societies. In recent years, there has been increasing concern about the erosion of democracy in the United States. This country's current political landscape faces, among other quandaries: district gerrymandering, voting restrictions disproportionately impacting marginalized populations, a vocal delegitimization of the electoral system on the part of a major political party, and historically low trust in the judicial system among the general public (Kulich & Iams Wellman, 2021).

As an emerging democracy, the signers of the Declaration of Independence and the Constitution of the United States were aware of the need to support the development of citizens. This has always been a complicated topic compelling philosophers, political scientists, and educators to interrogate the balance between individual freedoms and the need to foster a collective entity. As a case in point, once education became a public

DOI: 10.4324/9781003199106-2

service throughout the country, it quickly faced criticism of indoctrination from populations that did not ascribe to the overtly Protestant, English-speaking curriculum (Beadie & Burkholder, 2021). In this way, schooling has always been at the center of the democratic project in the United States.

Regardless of the plural opinions on what civic education in the United States looks like, so-called citizenship education has been a primary goal of schooling, and is considered a key element to the maintenance of democratic governing. Civic education, as it is conceived today, was properly articulated as a goal of public education in the United States during the Progressive Era, dating from the 1890s to 1920s. During a time of significant demographic shifts related to the urbanization of the American population and a high rate of immigration, the country experienced an emerging focus on the role of public education in fostering and maintaining a national identity. As Clark (2021) noted, the work of advocating for and, ultimately, crafting this portrayal of identity was articulated from the perspective of the demographic in power, "civic education at the turn of the century was all about preserving White, Protestant and Western European culture, and assimilating all-new city dwellers into this culture" (Clark, 2021, p. 19).

During the reform movement, Dewey described the commitment education should have toward civic agency, and how to achieve it. For Dewey, public schooling was less about cultivating a national identity, and more about developing and enacting democratic processes. His position argued for a version of experiential learning that integrated students into their communities in meaningful ways. In an essay from 1939 titled *Creative Democracy—The Task Before Us*, he claimed that to support a democratic form of governance, we must:

> realize in thought and act that democracy is a personal way of individual life; that it signifies the possession and continual use of certain attitudes, forming personal character and determining desire and purpose in all the relations of life. Instead of thinking of our own dispositions and habits as accommodated to certain institutions we have to learn to think of the latter as expressions, projections and extensions of habitually dominant personal attitudes.
>
> (Dewey, 2021, p. 62)

Dewey's contribution to civic education reminds us that democracy is not reproduced by teaching citizens to adhere to institutions. Instead, democracy is produced when citizens learn to enact, build, and construct democratic institutions. A central question for all educators, therefore, is: to what extent do schools allow for democratic participation?

In spite of the systemic inequities that persist in and at times are maintained by public education, schools continue to be a space of possibility for developing civic competencies. In their report, *The Civic Mission of Schools,* the Center for Information and Research on Civic Learning and Engagement (CIRCLE) observed, "schools are the only institutions with the capacity and mandate to reach virtually every young person in the country. Of all institutions, schools are the most systematically and directly responsible for imparting citizen norms" (Center for Information & Research on Civic Learning & Engagement, 2003, p. 5). In an increasingly polarized political climate, it is useful to remember that citizen norms are not tied to any political belief, but are dispositional tendencies that motivate people to participate, diagnose problems, and engage in the world. This thinking lays the groundwork for how contemporary academic and educational circles are thinking about a comprehensive approach to civics. One that centers the components of civic knowledge, values, and skills, all of which are integral to developing civic capacities. As we will explore in this chapter, this framework is important for understanding the breadth and complexity of the project of civic education.

The three-dimensional model of civic education

Civic instruction in the United States consolidated in the mid-1990s with the publication of two "origination documents" (Vontz, 1997, p. 6), the national standards and an assessment framework. The Center for Civic Education first published the *National Standards for Civics and Government* in 1994 and in 1996, and the National Assessment of Educational Progress (NAEP) developed a civics assessment to be administered every four years, to fourth, eighth, and twelfth graders. These documents overlap in an understanding of what is commonly known today as a three-dimensional model for civic education. Together, this model portrays civics curriculum as addressing: "civic knowledge, intellectual and participatory skills associated with citizenship, and dispositions related to responsible and humane citizenship" (Vontz, 1997, p. 6). Building on this model, recent scholarship suggested that to develop comprehensive civic education, "schools should take a broad view of citizenship education and prepare their students to acquire constructive civic skills and values as well as necessary civic knowledge" (Malin et al., 2014, p. 9). In a report on the status of civic education Vinnakota (2019) noted, "a new, improved system of civic education should be designed to produce citizens who are well-informed ... productively engaged in working for the common good ...; and hopeful about our democracy" (p. 8). When viewed together, we can subsume that education for civic engagement should do the following: build knowledge, foster democratic values that prompt students to act on this knowledge, and develop the skills needed for students to take action.

Contemporary civics curriculum draws on *The College, Career, and Civic Life (C3) Framework for Social Studies State Standards*, henceforth called the C3 Framework (NCSS, 2013). The C3 Framework introduces an overarching framework for social studies instruction. Here, standards scaffold learning outcomes by moving students through four dimensions, which function as consecutive stages of an inquiry process (the so-called Inquiry Arc). These dimensions of the framework refer to:

1 Developing questions and planning inquiries
2 Applying disciplinary tools and concepts (in civics, economics, geography, and history)
3 Evaluating sources and using evidence
4 Communicating conclusions and taking informed action.

As one of the core disciplines of social studies, civics curriculum is addressed in Dimension 2. For the discipline of civics, the standards specify, "civics is not limited to the study of politics and society; it also encompasses participation" (NCSS, 2013, p. 31). The civics discipline standards cover the role of citizens, historical social movements, and processes that are integral to democratic participation. They elaborate:

> In civics, students learn to contribute appropriately to public processes and discussions of real issues. Their contributions to public discussions may take many forms, ranging from personal testimony to abstract arguments. They will also learn civic practices such as voting, volunteering, jury service, and joining with others to improve society. Civics enables students not only to study how others participate, but also to practice participating and taking informed action themselves.
>
> (NCSS, 2013, p. 31)

The C3 Framework also frames preparedness for civic life as a main outcome of an effective social studies education; implying that civic engagement can be incorporated into instruction across the social studies. The standards state:

> Civic engagement in the social studies may take many forms, from making independent and collaborative decisions within the classroom, to starting and leading student organizations within schools, to conducting community-based research and presenting findings to external stakeholders ... In this respect, civic engagement is both a means of learning and applying social studies knowledge.
>
> (NCSS, 2013, p. 59)

The C3 Framework closely maps how a three-dimensional model of civics is not exclusively taught in civics courses. Important to our work, the standards suggest that civics must be addressed comprehensively throughout the entirety of the social studies curriculum. In this way, the key to teaching civic skills lies in the insistence that students engage in an arc of inquiry, which culminates in taking informed action.

While the support for a broad approach to civics is present in national standards, research finds this three-dimensional model is implemented inconsistently in schools. Shapiro and Brown (2018), in a survey of state civic curriculum, concluded, "no state currently provides sufficient and comprehensive civic education. . . [and] no states have experiential learning or local problem-solving components in their civics requirements" (pp. 2–5). This is largely due to programs focusing mainly on civic knowledge, resulting in a failure to implement the three-dimensional model. Hansen et al. (2018) analyzed state practices and concluded, "the most room for improvement lies in the incorporation of participatory and community engagement elements into state standards … [O]verall, policy lags behind the widely held view that these aspects of a civics education are essential" (p. 22). Conscious that state standards do not capture classroom practice, Hansen et al. (2018) also surveyed students about experiences in the classroom, finding that:

> civics education today still occurs, for many if not most students, through discussion rather than participation. … However … discussion alone is inadequate to provide students with the type of well-rounded civics education they need to prepare for lives as engaged and informed citizens.
>
> (p. 24)

So while there is a robust model for effective civic education within the C3 Framework, this model is complex and remains a stretch for most schools to implement. In contexts where civic education is under-resourced, what typically remains is a focus on content area knowledge, which covers the procedural and foundational understandings of how government and democratic systems work. This type of civic education is sometimes referred to as civic literacy (Milner, 2002). Following the three-dimensional model, civic literacy would be considered just one integral component of civic education. Despite it's one dimensionality, we note that civic literacy has been elevated within state standards. An example of this can be seen in our own state of Florida where, in 2019, the Department of Education introduced a civic literacy requirement for high school and postsecondary students. This requirement highlights the need to teach civic knowledge but does not focus on skills and values (Civic Literacy, n.d.). It is choices like these that narrow the interpretation of civic education and as a result, students in the United States continue to underperform in this area.

This underperformance is documented by the nation's report card which reported that less than one-quarter, or 24%, of 8th graders perform at or above proficiency on the NAEP exam (National Center for Education Statistics, 2018). Performance on this exam trends lower among Black (10% at or above proficiency), Hispanic (23% at or above proficiency), and Indigenous students (14% at or above proficiency), suggesting that Black, Indigenous, and people of color (BIPOC) students may have fewer opportunities for civic education. In spite of the recognized need for civic education and the extensive framework designed to teach it effectively,

> civic education as practiced in schools throughout the United States is not preparing students for effective participation in civic life. … Students are not finding inspiration in civic values as taught in schools today, nor are they gaining a sense that they are able to engage effectively in civic and political domains.
>
> (Malin et al., 2014, p. 7)

While data supporting quality civic education in schools is lacking, research does support the connections between quality civic instruction and increased student performance (Gill et al., 2018). The challenge then is finding ways to realize a three-dimensional model of civics instruction and create learning opportunities for democratic participation in schools, allowing students to develop their existing civic knowledge by putting civic values and skills to work.

Beyond civic literacy: Teaching civic skills and democratic values

Malin et al. (2014) noted that when schools place unequal weight on one component of civics, it can undermine the objectives of civic education entirely. As Beadie and Burkholder (2021) argued, presenting policy and political processes in an uncontested, value-neutral way strips them of their civic character. Not fulfilling the three-dimensional model of civics is not an anemic approach to civics, it is a hostile one that rids civics curriculum of values and actively works against engaged citizenship. To build civic skills and values back into the school curriculum, we must consider instructional practices, in particular those that allow the school to be a site for civic action. Ultimately, if schools are not themselves democratic institutions, they will fail at teaching democratic values and skills. As Stevenson (2011) noted,

> If what we mean by democracy includes the possibility of participation, listening, the capacity to change your mind or at least form an

opinion, cultural inclusion and a society where we can deliberate on roughly equal terms then this would suggest certain forms of education rather than others.

(p. 4)

If civic skills and values are to be gained in schools, we must pay attention to the way civics is taught, ensuring that the "choice of pedagogy is therefore the choice of the civic education model" (Wahrman & Hartaf, 2021, p. 4). The extent to which civic experiences are fostered within schools and are part of everyday classroom life is both integral to the success of civic education and a reflection of a three dimensional civics model (Hamilton & Kaufman, 2022). Two issues arise in relation to civic education pedagogies. The first concerns the type of pedagogical experiences students engage in; the second concerns the diverse and contested narrative around the possibilities for civic action in society, past and present. Regarding the first issue, civic education must continue to work across the three-dimensional model so that, as civic literacy is achieved, students have the opportunity to draw on this knowledge base when being called to deliberate and act. As suggested in the C3 Framework, civic competency is a practice that goes beyond acquiring knowledge, and must develop through the application of civic knowledge, values, and skills. The National Academy of Education (NAEd) reviewed the literature on effective civic instruction, and advanced the claim that civics can be applied through the dual actions of civic reasoning and discourse (Lee et al., 2021). Civic reasoning is prompted by the question: *what should we do?* This question carries within it a need to determine who the collective "we" is (who is included, who is excluded?), possible modes of action based on empirical understandings, and moral and ethical factors. Civic reasoning can lead to civic discourse, a deliberative process that asks students to grapple with multiple perspectives and objectives while building a collective response with peers. The NAEd report is careful to outline how all subject areas can create space for civic reasoning and discourse, reiterating that civic opportunities can arise outside of the social studies.

This kind of dialogic practice can, however, encounter roadblocks. Here, we consider a second factor that impacts civic education: the politicization of histories and experiences that challenge the White settler narrative of civic participation and citizenship. By ignoring structural and systemic differences that create barriers between civic knowledge and civic opportunities, traditional versions of civics curriculum can alienate students, particularly those students disproportionately impacted by structural and systemic inequity. More worrying is that this blindness is being written into educational policy. From January, 2021 to March, 2023, "44 states have introduced bills or taken other steps that would restrict teaching critical race theory or limit how teachers can discuss racism and sexism" (Schwartz, 2023, para. 5). While little evidence suggests that critical race theory is being taught in K-12 settings, these policies push schools to remove any critical theories or values from civic education on the grounds that such discussions teach students to hate the United States. When in reality, the removal of difference, critique, and criticism is a systematic way of reducing the value of civic education, and thus misinterpreting the goals of both a democratic society and the public school system. Supporting this, Banks (2017) found that students' experiences with civic education in schools can differ significantly, reporting that some students may not be, or may not feel, recognized as citizens. When school curriculum does not address the various ways concepts like civics, citizenship, and democracy show up in the real world, it prevents students from making meaningful connections between the curriculum and themselves. Meanwhile, as schools are narrowing their focus of civics to be only about civic knowledge, young people are receiving an increasingly expansive education in civics through their day-to-day interactions in the public sphere. As Clay and Rubin (2020) noted, "the manifestations of historical and systemic inequality dramatically shape the lived experience of citizenship for many Black and Brown young people. These experiences are, in themselves, 'civics lessons' that implicitly teach young people about the limitations of their citizenship" (p. 161). As Beadie and Burkholder (2021) documented, marginalized groups "have been forced to learn the basic terms and meaning (or meaning-lessness) of constitutional rights and protections in a way that dominant members of society have not" (p. 111). The result of a civics curriculum that is blind to the everyday life of civics is the emergence of a "contradictory citizenship model" (Wahrman & Hartaf, 2021, p. 4) where students may take civic courses without receiving a civic education.

The fourth dimension: Civic agency

If civic education aims to produce citizens that will maintain a working democracy, it must allow for difference and struggle. As Giroux (2005) noted, when citizenship "is removed from the terrain of historical contestation, it is also defined around a discourse of national unity and moral fundamentalism that drains from public life its most dynamic political and democratic possibilities" (p. 4). Levinson (2012) documented the difference between BIPOC and White students' political efficacy, finding evidence of a civic empowerment gap in the United States. She found that because civic processes in the United States are dominated by White, upper- and middle-class actors, students from all socio-economic and racial backgrounds require a civic education that explicitly addresses issues of inequality. Research supports tying civics curriculum to current issues facing our society (Levine & Kawashima-Ginsberg, 2017; Lo, 2020; Malin et al., 2014; Shapiro & Brown, 2018). Empirical studies show that taking up current events and controversial issues, engaging in a rich multitude of diverse sources (primary documents, local events, community speakers, and so on), and getting hands-on experiences all bring civic life into the classroom in impactful ways. Embracing the controversial nature of civic engagement is not only necessary, it is desirable. It allows civic education to provide opportunities for deliberation, problem-solving, and collective action, leading students to exercise civic agency. Westheimer (2020) concluded:

> well-functioning democratic society benefits from classroom practices that teach students to recognize ambiguity and conflict in factual content, to see human conditions and aspirations as complex and contested, and to embrace debate and deliberation as a cornerstone of democratic societies.
>
> (p. 10)

We find, therefore, that effective civic education must use all three of its branches: knowledge, skills, and values, in order to arrive at a fourth dimension, civic capacities (Vinnakota, 2019). Civic education is never complete without the application of civic agency, a way in which a collective body—like a classroom, school, or public community—work together on solving issues relevant to a common good. Under this assumption, Dewey's (2021) pragmatic vision for democratic education stands today:

> Democracy is the faith that the process of experience is more important than any special result attained, so that special results achieved are of ultimate value only as they are used to enrich and order the ongoing process. Since the process of experience is capable of being educative, faith in democracy is all one with faith in experience and education. All ends and values that are cut off from the ongoing process become arrests, fixations. They strive to fixate what has been gained instead of using it to open the road and point the way to new and better experiences.
>
> (p. 64)

Ultimately, civic education takes place in and around the subject area, just as it takes both in and around the classroom and school. To teach civics effectively, all educators must consider how their classrooms elicit processes of civic agency by embedding it in pedagogical relationships, the school community, and the everyday experiences of students.

Citizenship models

Civic education is synonymous with citizenship education. At the heart of civics is the figure of the citizen, which is a central component of policy and legislation. Civic education can support different models of citizenship. Westheimer and Kahne (2004) demonstrated that most educational approaches to citizenship correspond to one of three citizenship models. They described and illustrated the models in this way:

- *Personally responsible:* exercises citizenship through acting responsibly and volunteering. This citizenship model is character based, and values such character traits as honesty, obedience, and responsibility. EG— donates to a food drive.
- *Participatory:* exercises citizenship through long-term engagement with public collectives (community organizations, government, etc.). This citizen values problem solving and is part of democratic processes to support public services. EG—organizes a food drive.
- *Justice-oriented:* exercises citizenship through a critical interrogation of, and response to, systemic inequalities. While this model of citizenship is also participatory, engaging in processes that support civic life, it is deeply tied to a mission for making change. EG—explores the causes of food scarcity and develops plans to counter it.

Notably, of these three models, the first does not necessarily lead to the type of civic education that develops civic agency. For example, Thomson and Hall (2021) identify the configuration of the curriculum-citizen: "curriculum-citizens are recognised as universalised individuals with responsibilities. If they act responsibly, then citizens are accorded particular rights" (p. 32). This model of what citizenship looks like reinforces the model of personal responsibility, where, in practice, a citizen is thought of in terms of what they do. The personally responsible citizen has been critiqued for being the default citizenship model in schools. This model can be explicit, if a curriculum emphasizes governmental processes over democratic struggle, or implicit, if the school culture deemphasizes students' role as civic agents. As a strongly character-based vision of citizenship that focuses on getting along by following the rules, the model for a personally responsible citizen may:

> actually hinder rather than make possible democratic participation and change. For example, a focus on loyalty or obedience (common components of character education as well) works against the kind of critical reflection and action that many assume are essential in a democratic society.
>
> (Westheimer and Kahne, 2004, p. 244)

Participatory and justice-oriented citizenship models, on the other hand, are linked to approaches to civic education that attempt to maintain an emphasis on civic skills and values, with the ultimate goal of supporting civic capacities. Complicating this issue is the fact that citizenship models often reflect ideological frameworks. Smith (1997) documented how concepts of citizenship shift over time and align with political beliefs. This introduces conflict when developing and implementing civic education within the current climate of controversy and partisanship (Levinson, 2012). The work in this volume aligns itself with the capacity-oriented models of participatory and justice-oriented citizenship. Ultimately, we find across the literature, that calls for capacity building are essential to civic education. From the standards outlined across all four dimensions of the C3 Framework to recent empirical findings on how to improve equity in civic education (Lo, 2020), we identify a need for civic education to unapologetically support the development of participatory civic capacities in schools.

Cultural citizenship

The existence of different citizenship models suggests an understanding of citizenship that lies outside of political processes. While citizenship can be defined legally, it is also a mode of participation, within a classroom, a community, and beyond. As such, the very practice of citizenship undermines the universalistic language so often tied to democratic principles and policies. Some have suggested the term "cultural citizenship" (Ong, 1996; Pakulski, 1997; Stevenson, 2011) to frame citizenship beyond the legalistic language of rights. Citizenship as a cultural practice emphasizes the pathways through which people engage in and construct civil society. Here, the legal framework of rights is less determinant of citizenship than the processes (inclusions and exclusions) of participation. As Stevenson (2010) stated

> Cultural understandings of citizenship are not only concerned with "formal" processes, such as who is entitled to vote and the maintenance of an active civil society, but crucially with whose cultural practices are disrespected, marginalised, stereotyped and rendered invisible.
>
> (p. 276)

Cultural citizenship is a term that captures our cultural attachment to civic life; being a citizen involves building a sense of oneself as part society: "cultural citizenship is a dual process of self-making and being-made within webs of power linked to the nation-state and civil society" (Ong, 1996, p. 738). From a cultural perspective, the practice of citizenship is processual, social, and engages in movement both toward and against processes of individuation in the nation-state. The state may control who is a citizen, but what citizenship looks and feels like emerges through the everyday relationships and practices we take part in with others.

Citizenship as a cultural phenomenon operates as a mode of collective belonging; in turn, it becomes the process through which the civil sphere emerges from the social one. Stevenson's (2010, 2011) work on cultural citizenship depicted a form of citizenship that is a way to live a meaningful life with others, and a way to work toward better possible futures: "to be a cultural citizen means to engage in deliberative argument about who we might become, and to consider how we might lead virtuous and just lives in specific cultural locations and contexts" (Stevenson, 2010, p. 289). Cultural citizenship is not the result of policies or legal frameworks. Instead, it is built through collective action. If, in fact, cultural citizenship is a relational practice, then it could be conceived as a learning process. Delanty (2003) argued,

> citizenship is not entirely about rights or membership of a polity, but is a matter of participation in the political community and begins early in life. … it is about the learning of the self and of the relationship of self and other. It is a learning process in that it is articulated in perceptions of the self as an active agency and a social actor shaped by relations with others.
>
> (p. 602)

In an effort to reimagine who we may become, cultural citizenship serves as a reminder of the opportunities classrooms have to invite students into the type of deliberative arguments Stevenson cites. This reinforces the importance and potential of the role of civic agency within the classroom.

There is a tactile appeal in the malleable quality that the cultural sphere brings to our understanding of citizenship, as if the shape and form of citizenship was not entirely scripted but open to experimentation taking place in everyday decisions, interactions, and experiences. In this site of ambiguity, we locate an opening for cultural and artistic production to serve a unique purpose. To consider the role cultural production could have in supporting cultural citizenship we turn, finally, to the role of art education in relation to the project of civic education. Earlier in this chapter, we shared an essential prompt for engaging civic practice *vis a vis* the question: what should we do? Cultural citizenship is implicated both in the formation of the "we" as well as the visionary practice required to imagine a collective response to action. Pawley (2008) suggested that where cultural citizenship is concerned, culture is both a resource (informing citizenship, producing the "we") and a product (the outcome of citizen action and response). He stated, "in this analysis, the provision of cultural citizenship becomes a question of the effective regulation both of cultural product, and of access to it" (p. 600). Stevenson (2010) also advanced this argument, he understood that citizenship emerges from and is fed by cultural practices, which produce a shared understanding. He suggested: "citizens require an education and a media culture that is able to make sense of contemporary transformations and which offers citizens the space to share and critically interrogate diverse experiences and practices" (p. 289). Cultural citizenship's focus on the myriad ways in which we are bound together foregrounds the role of cultural practices; perhaps by intentionally aligning art education to cultural production, we can envision the way through which art education might position students as civic agents.

Cultural production

For art educators, the turn to culture is an invitation to consider the link between civic agency and cultural production. Gaztambide-Fernández (2013) described cultural production as encompassing "those practices, processes, and products involving symbolic creativity, some of which are sometimes associated—often in ways that are contested—with the concept of the arts" (p. 214). Thomson and Hall (2021) echoed the notion of symbolic creativity when they framed the relationship between art education and cultural production in reference to Fricker's (2007) concept of epistemic justice. In this light, participating in symbolic creativity can be framed as a right:

> The maintenance of heritage languages, artistic traditions, artefacts and architectures are vital to epistemic justice, but as important is the capacity to be seen to have a credible contribution to make to the processes of social meaning-making and their political, economic and legal enactment.
>
> (Thomson and Hall, 2021, p. 37)

Cultural production, Gaztambide-Fernández (2013) argued, is a cultural practice that young people need in order to participate in society. Suggesting, "rather than thinking about the arts as *doing something to people*, we should think about artistic forms as *something people do*" (Gaztambide-Fernández, 2013, p. 226), Gatzambide-Fernández used cultural production to frame artmaking within a practice of cultural citizenship.

Scholars have also bridged the relationship between cultural citizenship and arts education. Thomson and Hall (2021) and Kuttner (2015) considered how models of participatory and justice-oriented citizenship are located within arts education objectives. Kuttner saw the participatory cultural citizen as someone capable of "producing, remixing, and sharing original artistic works. She has a strong connection to her own cultural heritage, along with the freedom to explore new forms of expression and to share in cross-cultural exchange" (p. 76). The justice-oriented cultural citizen may "critically analyse the ways that the arts are implicated in processes of oppression and resistance" while activating cultural work in the service of activism (p. 76). Kuttner's application of citizenship models framed the civic contributions of cultural workers. Participatory cultural citizens use cultural forms to dialogue with, support, and evolve cultural practices; while justice-oriented cultural citizens use the arts to further a cause. Each framework can prompt art educators to ask questions about the citizenship model that lies at the heart of their curriculum.

Cultural production has been used to frame artistic and creative practices as an important, albeit informal, form of youth civic engagement (Gaztambide-Fernández & Matute, 2020; Hickey-Moody, 2015; Thomson et al., 2019). Hickey-Moody (2015) described youth arts practices as developing little publics, where participation gives rise to a form of aesthetic citizenship. To this end, "the materiality of [youth] arts practices constitutes a form of citizenship. What begins as affect, style, art practice, effects modes of community attachment that can influence community sentiment and can provide frameworks for policy and legislation" (*Parentheses added.* pp. 19–20). Hickey-Moody's description of little publics captured the civic significance of participation in art subcultures, and suggested aesthetic citizenship can be a mode through which civic life becomes possible for different groups of people, namely youth. Here, little publics give rise to "discrete forms of citizenship that are primarily articulated through feelings of belonging" (p. 26). In the informal and extracurricular projects she studied, Hickey-Moody found that even if citizenship is not the goal of arts programming, something about arts participation allows citizenship practices to develop. Hickey-Moody (2015) noted that emerging little publics are not necessarily aligned with a critical understanding of youth voice, whereby participation is equivalent to political agency. They are powerful because they frame artmaking as a process of cultural citizenship—that double practice of "self-making and being-made" (Ong, 1996, p. 738)—which has the potential to redefine the civic sphere of action that young people find themselves within. In other words, Hickey-Moody's aesthetic citizenship is an invitation to consider what new collective modes of being and belonging may emerge from art practices, which is a slightly different consideration than, say, interpreting arts practices from a pre-existing framework of citizenship models.

Hickey-Moody's (2015) work has precedent in cultural studies, which is an arena that asks what political significance emergent collectives, or little publics, may have. Hall (2016) argued that participation in cultural movements, specifically youth subcultures, is a way through which collective identity is developed. In a discussion of what subcultures offer people occupying a marginalized position in society, he suggested they provide to members

> a sense of themselves in the world; they have a pride of their place; they have a capacity to resist; they know when they are being abused by the dominant culture; and they have begun to know how to hold it at bay. But above all, they have a sense of some other person that they really are. They have become visible to themselves.
>
> (p. 204)

Hall framed the so-called little publics that emerge through cultural practice as civic spaces, in the sense that they build a new collective identity. Participation in them is not one of recognition but one of becoming, of joining in, of creating yourself anew with others. Hall theorized,

> people have to have a language to speak about where they are and what other possible futures are available to them. These futures may not be real; if you try to concretise them immediately, you may find there is nothing there. But what is there, what is real, is the possibility of being someone else, of being in some other social space from the one in which you have already been placed.
>
> (p. 205)

Civic education aims to give young people access to modes of participation in civic life. Cultural production suggests that as new practices emerge, we continue to discover what civic participation looks like. Symbolic creativity may not follow the critical understanding of participatory or justice-oriented citizenship. It may, however, come to support these practices by first positioning students as part of something, a something which they may later feel called to advocate for, or within. Because cultural production operates through modes of intensity and pleasure, it captivates participants in unexpected and potentially unarticulated ways.

Taking up cultural production as the work of art education, Gaztambide-Fernandez (2013) suggested the field of art education does not need to be concerned with how art practice impacts students. Instead, he asked, what are they doing with art? We extend this by returning to the question of what should we do? What should art education do to support students' cultural citizenship? What should students be doing with art, if they want to transform themselves or the world?

Emergent citizenship through cultural production

Hickey-Moody's (2015) discussion of aesthetic citizenship considered the relationship between the affective and political registers. Rather than sever the connection between the cultural sphere and the civic one, she bridged them: "cultural systems are altered through affect. Policies, institutionalized practices, and modes of spatial organization effected by institutionalized practices, are shifted as the result of affective allegiances" (p. 129). Cultural citizenship, enacted through cultural production, demonstrates that civics can take place outside the bounds of politics and policy. This type of practice may be suspect for the project of civic education, because this sphere of culture is not inherently political:

> Cultural forms themselves are important. They create the possibility of new subjectivities, but they do not themselves guarantee their progressive or reactionary content. They still require social and political practices to articulate them to particular political positions.
>
> (Hall, 2016, p. 197)

In response, we would argue that although little publics may not constitute a political identity, they are necessary for political identity to form. Affective allegiances are the grounds for political affiliation, thus, cultural forms may not be political, per se, but political action relies on them as a foundation for generating motivations and responses. Hickey-Moody (2015) concluded, "taste and culture are forms of affective pedagogy that young people mobilize to make social and political possibilities" (p. 120).

The cultural sphere is one of possibility and emergence. As Hall and other scholars from cultural studies have documented, the unpredictable potential of cultural forms to impact politics is what makes the cultural realm so powerful. Because it is captivating, desiring, and fluid in a way that policy can never hope to be, it opens up possibilities for transformation. While working in a framework dominated by civic standards, malleability can be forgotten. This is an obstacle to developing an affective and effective civic education. Giroux (2005), echoing Dewey's investment in democratic processes, reminded us:

> Citizenship, like democracy itself, is part of a historical tradition that represents a terrain of struggle over the forms of knowledge, social practices, and values... However, it is not a term that has any transcendental significance outside the lived experiences and social practices of individuals who make up diverse forms of public life. Once we acknowledge the concept of citizenship as a socially constructed historical practice, it becomes all the more imperative to recognize

that categories like citizenship and democracy need to be problematized and reconstructed for each generation.

(p. 5)

Art education is well prepared to engage in civic education by activating modes of cultural production that draw unexpected but powerful connections between materials and events, histories and the present, schools and communities, students and the world. By drawing on participatory and justice-oriented models of cultural citizenship, we suggest that a civically engaged art education is possible.

References

Americans' Views of Government: Decades of Distrust, Enduring Support for Its Role. (2022, June 6). Pew Research Center. https://www.pewresearch.org/politics/2022/06/06/americans-views-of-government-decades-of-distrust-enduring-support-for-its-role/

Banks, J. A. (2017). Failed citizenship and transformative civic education. *Educational Researcher*, 46(7), 366–377. https://doi.org/10.3102/0013189X1772674

Beadie, N., & Burkholder, Z. (2021). From the diffusion of knowledge to the cultivation of agency: A short history of civic education policy and practice in the United States. In, C. D. Lee, G. White, D. Dong (Eds.), *Educating for civic reasoning and discourse*. National Academy of Education. https://naeducation.org/educating-for-civic-reasoning-and-discourse/

Center for Information & Research on Civic Learning & Engagement (CIRCLE). (2013). Civic learning through action: The case of generation citizen. *Tufts University*. http://www.civicyouth.org/wp-content/uploads/2013/07/Generation-Citizen-Fact-Sheet-July-1-Final.pdf

Civic literacy. (n.d.). Florida Department of Education. https://www.fldoe.org/civicliteracy/

Clark, J. S. (2021). *Local civics with national purpose: Civic education origins at Shortridge high school*. Palgrave Macmillan.

Clay, K. L., & Rubin, B. C. (2020). "I look deep into this stuff because it's a part of me": Toward a critically relevant civics education. *Theory & Research in Social Education*, 48(2), 161–181. https://doi.org/10.1080/00933104.2019.1680466

Delanty, G. (2003). Citizenship as a learning process: Disciplinary citizenship versus cultural citizenship. *International Journal of Lifelong Education*, 22(6), 597–605. https://doi.org/10.1080/0260137032000138158

Dewey, J. (2021). *America's public philosopher: Essays on social justice, economics, education, and the future of democracy*. E. T. Weber (Ed.). Columbia University Press.

Foa, R. S., & Mounk, Y. (2016). The danger of deconsolidation: The democratic disconnect. *Journal of Democracy*, 27(3), 5–17. https://doi.org/10.1353/jod.2016.0049

Fricker, M. (2007). *Epistemic injustice. Power and the ethics of knowing*. Oxford University Press.

Gaztambide-Fernández, R., & Matute, A. A. (2020). *Cultural production and participatory politics*. Routledge.

Gaztambide-Fernández, R. (2013). Why the arts don't "do" anything: Toward a new vision for cultural production in education. *Harvard Educational Review, 83*(1), 211–237. https://doi.org/10.17763/haer.83.1.a78q39699078ju20

Gill, B., Tilley, C., Whitesell, E., Finucane, M., Potamites, L., & Corcoran, S. (2018). *The impact of democracy prep public schools on civic participation: Final report*. Mathematica Policy Research.

Giroux, H. (2005). *Schooling and the struggle for public life: Democracy's promise and education's challenge*. Routledge.

Hall, S. (2016). *Cultural studies 1983: A theoretical history*. J. Slack, & L. Grossberg (Eds.). Duke University Press. https://doi.org/10.1515/9780822373650

Hamilton, L. S., & Kaufman, J. H. (2022). Indicators of equitable civic learning in U.S. public schools. *Educational Assessment, 27*(2), 187–196. 10.1080/10627197.2022.2087623

Hansen, M., Levesque, E., Valant, J., & Quintero, D. (2018). *The 2018 Brown Center report on American education: How well are American students learning?* The Brown Center on Education Policy, Brookings Institute. https://www.brookings.edu/multi-chapter-report/the-2018-brown-center-report-on-american-education/

Hickey-Moody, A. (2015). *Youth, arts, and education. Reassembling subjectivity through affect*. Routledge.

Kulich, C., & Iams Wellman, E. (2021). *The United States has a democracy problem: What democratic erosion scholarship tells us about January 6*. Items: Insights from the Social Sciences. https://items.ssrc.org/democracy-papers/the-united-states-has-a-democracy-problem-what-democratic-erosion-scholarship-tells-us-about-january-6/

Kuttner, P. J. (2015). Educating for cultural citizenship: Reframing the goals of arts education. *Curriculum Inquiry, 45*(1), 69–92. https://doi.org/10.1080/03626784.2014.980940

Lee, C. D., White, G., & Dong, D. (Eds.) (2021). *Educating for civic reasoning and discourse*. National Academy of Education. https://naeducation.org/educating-for-civic-reasoning-and-discourse/

Levine, P., & Kawashima-Ginsberg, K. (2017). *The republic is (still) at risk—and civics is part of the solution*. Jonathan M. Tisch College of Civic Life, *Tufts University*. https://www.civxnow.org/sites/default/files/resources/SummitWhitePaper.pdf

Levinson, M. (2012). *No citizen left behind*. Harvard University Press. https://doi.org/10.4159/harvard.9780674065291

Levinson, M. (2014). Action civics in the classroom. *Social Education, 78*, 68–72. https://www.ingentaconnect.com/content/ncss/se/2014/00000078/00000002/art00005

Lo, J. (Ed.). (2020). *Equity in civic education* [White paper]. Generation Citizen and iCivics. https://civxnow.org/wp-content/uploads/2021/08/Equity-in-Civic-Eduation-White-Paper_Public.pdf

Malin, H., Ballard, P. J., Attai, M. L., Colby, A., Damon, W., Banks, J. A., Hahn, C. L., Hess, D., Hess, F. M., Liu, E., Moran, R., & Suárez-Orozco, M. (2014). Youth Civic Development & Education. In, *Stanford Center on Adolescence Conference* (pp. 1–24). Center on Adolescence and Center for Multicultural Education. https://coa.stanford.edu/youth-civic-development-education

Milner, H. (2002). *Civic literacy: How informed citizens make democracy work.* University Press of New England.

National Center for Education Statistics [NCESS]. (2018). Results from the 2018 civics, geography, and U.S. history assessments. U.S. Department of Education. Institute of Education Sciences. https://www.nationsreportcard.gov/highlights/civics/2018/

NCSS (National Council for the Social Studies) (2013). *College, career & civic life (C3) framework for social studies state standards: Guidance for enhancing the rigor of k-12 civics, economics, geography, and history.* National Council for the Social Studies.

Ong, A. (1996). Cultural citizenship as subject-making. Immigrants negotiate racial and cultural boundaries in the United States. *Current Anthropology, 37*(5), 737–62. https://doi.org/10.1086/204560

Pakulski, J. (1997). Cultural citizenship. *Citizenship Studies, 1*(1), 73–86. https://doi.org/10.1080/13621029708420648

Pawley, L. (2008). Cultural citizenship. *Sociology Compass, 2*(2), 594–608. https://doi.org/10.1111/j.1751-9020.2008.00094.x

Schwartz, S. (2023, March 23). Map: Where critical race theory is under attack. *Education Week.* https://www.edweek.org/policy-politics/map-where-critical-race-theory-is-under-attack/2021/06

Shapiro, S., & Brown, C. (2018). *The state of civics education.* Center for American Progress. https://www.americanprogress.org/issues/education-k-12/reports/2018/

Smith, R. (1997). *Civic ideals: Conflicting visions of citizenship in U.S. History.* Yale University Press.

Stevenson, N. (2010). Cultural citizenship, education and democracy: Redefining the good society. *Citizenship Studies, 14*(3), 275–291. https://doi.org/10.1080/13621021003731823

Stevenson, N. (2011). *Education and cultural citizenship.* Sage.

Thomson, P., & Hall, C. (2021). Beyond civics: Art and design education and the making of active/activist citizens. In N. Addison & L. Burgess (Eds.), *Debates in art and design education* (pp. 31–44). Routledge.

Thomson, P., Hall, C., Earl, L., & Geppert, C. (2019). Towards an arts education for cultural citizenship. In S. Riddle & M. Apple (Eds.), *Re-imagining education for democracy* (pp. 174–189). Routledge.

Vinnakota, R. (2019). *From Civic Education to a Civic Learning Ecosystem: A Landscape Analysis and Case for Collaboration* [Research Report]. Red and Blue Works. https://rbw.civic-learning.org/wp-content/uploads/2019/12/CE_online.pdf

Vontz, T. (1997). *Strict scrutiny: An analysis of national standards on civic education through the perspective of contemporary theorists.* Indiana University.

Wahrman, H., & Hartaf, H. (2021). Are schools educating toward active citizenship? The internal school struggle between contradictory citizenship models. *Education, Citizenship and Social Justice, 16*(1), 3–16. https://doi.org/10.1177/1746197919859993

Westheimer, J. (2020). Can education change the world? *Kappa Delta Pi Record, 56*(1), 6–12. https://doi.org/10.1080/00228958.2020.1696085

Westheimer, J., & Kahne, J. (2004). What kind of citizen? The politics of educating for democracy. *American Educational Research Journal, 41*(2), 237–269.

2   Teaching Civics through Art

Nearly a half century ago, education philosopher Elliot Eisner charged that art educators were generally too fixated on art of the past (Eisner, 1972). Since then, many art education practitioners and thought leaders have focused on "the now" by producing art curriculum based on contemporary art practices, present-day social issues, and new technologies and visualities. If the past and the present are useful frames for developing art curriculum, then what happens when we focus on "the next"? How might we think about art curriculum of the future?

(Kraehe, 2020, p. 4)

The field of art education has volleyed around a myriad of ways to explain or identify the arts' value in and out of schools (Bolin, 2020; Carpenter & Tavin, 2010; Kraehe, 2020). While the names attached to art education have shifted throughout the years, Dewey's assertion that democratic values are central to the ways we function in our day-to-day lives remains central to art education's relevance in schools (Blandy, 2011; Dewey, 2011). Blandy extends this to remind art educators that "democracy as a way of life, with a primary goal of education being to prepare people to participate in this way of life to the greatest extent possible" should be simultaneously a point of departure and arrival in conversations about the potential for art education (p. 252). In Chapter 1, we argued that a model of cultural citizenship can help art educators reframe their understanding of young people's artmaking in terms of civic participation. This then is where we begin to see the relevance of the arts and the potential application of democratic values and civic engagement in art education. We are not alone in this assumption; while often called different names, the appearance of civic outcomes via community engagement occurs over and over again in the literature mapping the field of art education.

For the last 20 years art education has been moving "toward a profoundly critical, historical, political, and self-reflective understanding of visual culture and social responsibility" (Carpenter & Tavin, 2010,

DOI: 10.4324/9781003199106-3

p. 329). This shift asks art educators to move away from thinking of the work of art as just representation or interpretation and toward an art education that facilitates a mode of cultural production that reaches outside of classrooms and holds at its core the relevance of students' lives, communities, and histories (Gaztambide-Fernandez, 2013). Further, in light of young people's demonstrated interest in activism, and their gravitation toward cultural and artistic production in the service of this activism, we posit that art education can support their endeavors through the development of civics curricula grounded in artistic thinking and researching. We are interested in how creative inquiry and artmaking catalyze movement into communities and civic life.

This chapter explores how art and civics overlap with specific attention to the ways art education is already doing this work. It discusses how art educators may draw on civic education to design a curriculum that centers young people, their communities, interests, and artmaking as they explore and expand their notion of what civic participation might look like. As such, we are most interested in reviewing models of art education that are aligned with the outcomes of civic education. In this review of literature, we look at community-based art education (Lawton et al., 2019; London, 1994; Stephens, 2006; Ulbricht, 2005); service learning in art education (Alexander, 2015; Buffington, 2007; Eckhoff, 2011; Hutzel et al., 2010); socially engaged/interventionist art education (Hyungsook, 2014; Powell & Lajevic, 2011; Rollins, 2019; Schlemmer et al., 2017); place-based art education (Anderson & Suominen Guyas, 2012; Bertling, 2015; Blandy & Hoffman, 1993; Graham, 2007; Inwood, 2008; Sobel, 1997; Trafí-Prats, 2012); and critical pedagogy in art education (Acuff, 2018; Bell, 2010; Desai, 2010; Kraehe & Acuff, 2013; Mernick, 2021.; Stuhr et al., 2008).

The sections that follow seek to identify the connecting threads that weave across these contemporary pedagogical and curricular trends. In doing this, we are not trying to reinvent art education, but rather to identify what art education is already doing that might serve to create clear lines to the future-oriented work of an artistically engaged model of civic education. We see this literature review as charting the possibilities for a civically engaged art education by recognizing exemplary theoretical, pedagogical, and empirical conceptualizations from the field. For the purpose of this literature review, we limited our sources to the last 20 years, with the only exceptions being the work of London (1994), who laid the foundation for a conceptualization of art education as pivotal to communities. We have looked across these theoretical and pedagogical trends to identify the core values and qualities we believe are central to a civically engaged art education. In the sections that follow, we explore an art education that is school-centered, locally bound, historically relevant, inherently critical, self-reflexive, collaboratively conceived, socially involved, and most importantly, future-oriented.

School-centered

We begin our exploration of the possibilities that arts education might offer civic engagement in schools by looking at a model of schooling where physical school buildings and the art classrooms inside of them are central to students' lives. Much of the art education literature on community-based learning positions young people in learning environments outside of schools, advocating for a version of art education that opens up possibilities for connected learning that takes place in and alongside communities (Peppler et al., 2022; Ulbricht, 2005). This model of informal schooling is important to the lives of young people, but in seeking ways to engage students in generative and extended conversations about civics, we see extended time as critical. Students need the opportunity to engage in recurring explorations of civic knowledge, skills, and values to be able to move toward the even more complex processes of civic engagement and participation. While informal educational settings offer the potential to function outside the structures of K-12 environments, we see the inherent repetition and recurrence that the K-12 calendar offers as necessary for this type of learning. Rollins (2019) explores this as he recounts his long-term engagement with the Kids of Survival (KOS) saying:

> Art outside of the classroom is essential, and surely more convenient. But all of my instincts as an artist, educator, and citizen impel me to devise plans that will … renew partnerships with public schools … Our alternative pedagogy is not to offer an alternative, but rather to do everything in our power to respectfully advocate for positive pedagogical change in art education within the so-called mainstream classroom, especially in the public schools.
>
> (Rollins, 2019, p. 88)

The art education we envision prioritizes the school experience by highlighting its potential to be a transformative moment in young people's trajectories. As a shared space, schools bring together large numbers of young people to learn alongside one another. Furthering this line of thinking, we consider the space the art room provides. Art classrooms, and the teachers in them, are often overlooked in a system where effectiveness is determined through standardization and conformity. While the history of art education shows an eagerness to be legitimized through standardization, the field persists and thus resists by remaining fluid and changing (Bolin, 2020). Coats (2020) conceptualizes this as an indiscernibility, saying "[t]here is a freedom in being indiscernible—not necessarily invisible or hidden but undefined. Being open creates porous edges, inviting new connections and allowing transformation to occur more easily" (p. 45). Like Coats, we argue that perhaps being overlooked and underestimated might make art teachers perfect candidates for the subversive work of teaching toward civic participation. In a way, the lack of attention and standardization allows for flexibility in the ways that teachers interpret what teaching and learning about art should look like. This openness creates room to move and even linger in inquiry processes. A model of art education advocating for the extended exploration of a specific theme or idea over the course of a semester or term lets students spend time with their thoughts and ideas (Boughton, 2004; Graham, 2019; Taylor et al., 2006). While this shared space and time are critical in providing opportunities for deep engagement with topics, a civically engaged art education also relies on the local to provide starting points for students to inquire into the ways their communities support or diminish their civic potential.

Locally bound

While we see the importance of schools serving as a community touchstone, we have also thought about how schools are positioned in relationship to the community. Although the emergence of charter schools, school choice, and rezoning impacts the relationship between the school's physical location and the populations of students in attendance, we still believe that schools can serve as a vital life source in civic ecosystems. "Each state, city, and even neighborhood has its own particular civic ecosystem—so much so that a general description of the state of civic learning in our country (beyond the basic observation that it bears improving) is of little value" (Vinnakota, 2019, p. 12). In viewing communities as civic ecosystems, cultural, social, political, and ecological conditions merge to create a specific place-based identity that might be called a bioregional perspective (Blandy, 2011; Childs, 2001). If we see schools as central to civic ecosystems and primary contributors to bioregional perspectives, the convergence of the values from place-based and community-based art education becomes a way of thinking about schools, and art classrooms, as key locales for students to learn about. When this kind of focus occurs, we see student outcomes that provide evidence of young people's agential development. This supposition is supported through investigations into art education projects that explore cities as urban landscapes of possibility and hope where art education presents "a pedagogical stance that stands against the tendency to shape young people to serve the needs of the status quo" (Hutzel et al., 2012, p. 1). Art education literature also brings attention to "rural areas, where teachers, parents and community members should be involved actively in developing arts programs that build upon local resources and histories" (Clark & Zimmerman, 2000, p. 34). This work highlights the need for local context not just in urban environments but also in rural environments by illustrating the deep relevance of local histories and contexts regardless of geographical location. Essentially arguing that all places have local communities and that art education should do the work of engaging them in ways that blur the lines between knowledge found inside and outside of classrooms.

By highlighting the importance of viewing young people as community members and positioning their experiences and learning about local communities at the center of the art classroom, art educators contribute to the sustainability of art classrooms, schools, and the communities they are situated in. "What I think the concept of sustainability is promising for the arts and art education is that there is a growing recognition that a sustainable environment is possible only if 'culture' is viewed as integral to quality of life" (Blandy, 2011, p. 245). This expands the traditional notions of sustainable ecological environments to include how educational practices contribute to sustaining the specific lives of communities from an ecological, cultural, and social perspective (Ball & Lai, 2006; Graham, 2007; Inwood, 2008). This model of sustainable art education brings together public schools and communities to build connections and partnerships that begin in the art classroom, but have the potential to continue once students leave school (Bolin, 2020). The literature surrounding an art education of place makes clear the impact the arts can have on local communities and highlights the importance of centering communities as rich material resources that transcend the financial barriers that art educators often face. This relocation of the community from the periphery of art classrooms to the center, brings with it the community and all its resources as materials for students' artmaking (Gray & Graham, 2007; London, 1994). For example, an oral history recording, historical photograph, student memory, and city map might serve as the foundation for artmaking that asks what happens when the people, places, and events that make up the living history of a community become fodder for artistic inquiry and practice?

Historically relevant

In contemporary life, a sense of community is often splintered by the inexorable forces of the global economy and mass media. Places are owned, used up, and thrown aside. In the process, the sense of belonging to a particular community is lost. Many Americans have not developed a connection to the place where they live on which they can build an ethic of care and responsibility. Place-based education aims to counter the restless separation of people from the land and their communities by grounding learning in local phenomena and personal experiences.

(Gray & Graham, 2007, p. 302)

When considering a locally bound, civically engaged art classroom, we find resonance in the work of community-based art educators as they argue for a vision of art education that holds students central but also asks young people to position themselves in relationship to what London (1994) refers to as "ever-widening circles of experience" (p. 33). While we have argued that these circles include local communities, educators must also look at the historical narratives and the related memories of local spaces. These narratives, traditions, memories, archives, and artifacts create a foundation for understanding the nuances of local communities and provide context for young people to do the deeply introspective work of positioning themselves as agential beings within communities (Bey, 2013). Regardless of school and community locations being categorized as urban or rural, the surrounding resources, when conceptualized as people, places, and events, provide a glimpse at how historical narratives actively shape the places young people live in (Clark & Zimmerman, 2000; Hutzel et al., 2012; Powell, 2008). "These spaces must be reactivated as gardens for planting metaphors where teachers, students, and community members alike can weave narratives and reap lost legacies" (Bey, 2013, p. 20).

Building out of a vision for art education as interested and invested in the historical narratives of people, places, and events, we believe a civically engaged art curriculum must do more than just position students in relationship to local histories. Instead, it should ask young people to begin to see the ways they are being formed by these histories. An art education that is historically relevant invites teachers and students to learn about community histories through an exploration of local sites, oral histories, and archival documents. The real value in this approach to art education is that it draws significant connections between then and now, highlighting the ways in which history often predicts and determines the present. In this process, young people come to understand that knowing history allows for informed disruption of the present. This means as art teachers teach and learn through critical moments of local histories, they must move beyond questions of who am I? and where do I come from?, to include questions of what community shapes me? and, what should we do, moving forward? A civically engaged art education posits that by doing the work of historians, we ask young people to juxtapose and situate their identities within a web of complex socio-cultural-political moments spanning the past and present and, in response, begin to critically understand themselves and their potential in relation to others (Kraehe, 2018).

Inherently critical

What is required is a critical consciousness, an informed awareness of the social forces which oppress our lives, confine our growth, and define our dreams, and an additional awareness of what we can do to combat them ... to clarify the ways in which the social, political, and economic worlds work and how it can be improved.

(Lanier, 1976, p. 20, as cited in Duncum, 2018)

The drive to belong and relate to one another serves as a foundational value in a critically imagined view of art education. Critical multiculturalism is one way that art education has envisioned centering criticality in the classroom. This educational model envelopes "various critical theoretical threads such as anti-racist education, critical race theory, and critical pedagogy" (Ballengee-Morris, 2019, p. 81). Critical multicultural art education acknowledges the necessity of applying critical thinking skills to understand the far-reaching implications for colonial practices. Ballengee-Morris (2019) argued that the investigation of history and culture are central to understanding "prejudice, discrimination, and colonialism" (p. 81). An investigation of self and others is necessary to understand injustice and find ways of envisioning alternate futures. Like critical multiculturalism, critical pedagogy in art education holds four key pedagogical tenets central: the political nature of knowledge, the democratic nature of teaching and learning, the centrality of social change, and the importance of students' lived experiences (Dyer, 2021).

Building out of the foundation of critical pedagogy, we add that at the core of criticality is the degree with which a young person is able to engage in social empathy (Wagaman, 2011). Social empathy has been argued to be a core component for achieving social justice. This view of transformative, justice-oriented education is achieved through empathetic understanding, contextual grounding, and ultimately social responsibility. In this definition of social empathy, it is important to note that criticality as a pedagogical tool to develop empathy is not

premised on taken for granted assumptions about care, concern and sympathy towards the other, but rather inspires modes of affective perspective-taking and affective practices that call subjects (e.g., teachers, students, parents) into account for their own complicity in perpetuating coloniality.

(Zembylas, 2018, p. 405)

Critical approaches to social empathy and responsibility provide a foundation for understanding civic education (see Chapter 1). Thus, we see criticality as the ability to engage in the development of self, in relation to others, grounded in historical and contemporary contexts, with the goal of nurturing a sense of social commitment and obligation.

In line with this thinking, Dewhurst (2010, 2011) argued for a vision of social justice art education that holds central the importance of process as an inherently critical activity. Drawing from the scholarship surrounding social justice art education, we see great value in a vision of art education that "shares a commitment to create art that draws attention to, mobilizes action towards, or attempts to intervene in systems of inequality or injustice" (Dewhurst, 2010, p. 7). She claimed that social justice art does not have to be inherently political, saying, "as long as the *process* of making art offers participants a way to construct knowledge, critically analyze an idea, and take action in the world, then they are engaged in a practice of social justice artmaking" (Dewhurst, 2010, p. 8). By conceiving the surrounding world as inherently relational, Dewhurst (2010) opened up possibilities for enacting critical pedagogical practices that move beyond issues of inequity to include any realm of our social world that impacts students directly. While the cornerstone of action or impact appears in literature surrounding social justice art education, it is important to highlight that without relevance and critique, the work's impact almost always falls flat (Dewhurst, 2010).

Art education must heed this warning by ensuring that the work of making and the artwork itself are carefully delineated to ensure that teachers see their role in the classroom not as the creator of the project, but rather as the facilitator of a transformative experience. López et al. (2017) put forward a pedagogy for change framework and noted the necessity for the exploration of self within a larger cultural and historical framework. The work of positioning student and teacher identities in context works from an asset-based framework where students' experiences bring relevant and critical information into the art room and the job of the teacher is to facilitate the work of connecting these experiences to larger social, political, and cultural narratives or realities (López et al., 2017). Conceptualizing a vision of art education that is inherently critical requires educators and students to always be in a process of critical engagement, reflection, and exploration. To do this art educators must acknowledge the centrality of student experiences and recognize the knowledge produced through these personal stories as foundational to student engagement (Acuff, 2018).

Art education must also bring into focus epistemological ideals from outside the mainstream White norm typically found in K-12 schools. By doing the work of opening up perspectives, art teachers might ask their students to question the status quo through arts-based investigations of history, paying close attention to what is not present in archives and institutional memories of people, places, and events (Acuff, 2018; Bell & Desai, 2011). Bell and Desai (2011) clarify this criticality as it relates to the art room by reminding us that art classrooms must ask students and teachers to not just investigate the "systems of oppression" (p. 288) but to expand this by positioning student narratives within, alongside, and in relation to the social, cultural, and political context that shapes them (Acuff, 2018). "Often young people are not given sufficient opportunities to practise critical, collaborative and self-reflective acts of learning about belonging in multicultural societies" (Habib, 2019, p. 179). This becomes the challenge when envisioning an art education that is inherently critical, one that recognizes that criticality as an end is not enough. While necessary, the term criticality does not always imply a collaborative engagement between teachers and students to examine and imagine a different reality (Quinn, 2021). This orientation toward the future becomes the next foundational concept in our imagining of a civically engaged art education.

Future oriented

The ability to imagine our world differently through the arts, is critical for understanding future orientation as a goal of civically engaged art education (Greene, 1995). We note here that future orientation is not enough, instead students must be asked to move their projects toward the future by finding ways to share them outwardly and begin the process of enacting the change that was imagined (Dewhurst, 2010). This may be uncomfortable for some art teachers, because by first designing curricular opportunities that are responsive to contemporary issues and then later presenting that work to the public as possibilities for change, teachers open up their classrooms, students, and themselves to critique. Unless the outcome is an exhibition or arts night celebration, this kind of educational transparency is often seen as too engaged, opinionated, or liberal.

Using the arts to expand and explore alternate realities that reimagine futures as more socially just is a lofty goal, especially when artmaking is often viewed as an independent task, with collaborative activity occurring after the student has created their piece and displays it in the hallway or community for others to view. However, we advocate for the notion of collaboration as integral to the entire teaching and learning process. This notion of collaboration then moves outside of just the classroom to include community collaborations. This is a concept grounded in the writing on social justice art education that advocates for education that "moves away from doing things *for* people and towards doing things in solidarity *with* them" (Quinn et al., 2012, p. 217). To be able to move into this realm of doing something with art, established in Chapter 1 as the goal of a three-dimensional civic education, students and teachers must engage in planning that is "collaborative, reciprocal, and contextual" (Dewhurst, 2010, p. 11).

What makes this approach different is that students simultaneously help design the curriculum and benefit from the outcomes. This type of planning and investment looks different depending on the location of the school, the histories of the students, and the varied ways these two factors interact. This means that curriculum in rural areas will look, feel, and happen differently than in urban areas. Despite differences in location, a focus on collaboratively reimagining the future in both project development and dissemination is a marker of civically engaged art education. We believe that the negotiation of a classroom community through collectively conceived objectives or outcomes helps teachers and students move toward a more complex reimagining of the future with stakeholders, organizations, and even policy makers (Clark & Zimmerman, 2000; Dewhurst, 2010).

Conclusion

When students and teachers work together to conceive of projects, outcomes, and impact, the entirety of an educational experience is shaped by the iterative processes of mentoring, participation, collective discussion, and large-scale problem solving (Blandy, 2011). Blandy reminds us that participatory culture is central to the ways that young people are already engaging with one another. Since his 2011 publication, this reality has only become more apparent as we watch young people stitch, re-tweet, and share across social media platforms. What then is the role of the art teacher? According to Blandy, the art educator is responsible for introducing and facilitating ways for young people to enact participation. Presenting young people with opportunities to practice "play, performance, simulation, appropriation, multitasking, distributed cognition, collective intelligence, judgment, transmedia navigation, networking, and negotiation" (p. 250). This means the role of the teacher and student must shift drastically as we imagine the future of art education differently. Where the material processes of painting and drawing might be replaced by more contemporary artistic devices like sound or video. Where the goals of the art classroom shift away from just learning the elements and principles, toward outcomes like building community and fostering dialogue (Duncombe, 2016).

A future orientation for arts education might be imagining a classroom where gridded murals are replaced with community initiatives, and the spotlight on the arts night is transformed into cultural happenings (Clark & Zimmerman, 2000). Whatever the shift may be, the world of art education is ready for it. We believe that envisioning art education as civically engaged might be one way of bridging the gap between the contemporary art world and the aims of art education for social justice. We believe that schools offer the potential to scaffold and nurture social empathy over the lifespan of young people's educational journeys. We believe that the local environment young people live in should be central to understanding both civics and art, and that our neighborhoods, towns, cities, and counties hold hidden histories that might help connect youth to their communities. Through these community connections, classrooms can begin to teach civic participation, activating various versions of history and inviting students to engage in critical research practices that center around a collective story of communities. Finally, we believe that this model of art education must work collaboratively toward imagining a future that while not yet possible, is entirely attainable.

References

Acuff, J. B. (2018). 'Being' a critical multicultural pedagogue in the art education classroom. *Critical Studies in Education, 59*(1), 35–53. https://doi.org/10.1080/17508487.2016.1176063.

Alexander, A. (2015). Engaging a developmentally disabled community through arts-based service-learning. *Journal of Higher Education Outreach and Engagement, 19*(4), 183–206.

Anderson, T., & Suominen Guyas, A. (2012). Earth education, interbeing, and deep ecology. *Studies in Art Education, 53*(3), 223–245. https://doi.org/10.1080/00393541.2012.11518865

Ball, E. L., & Lai, A. (2006). Place-based pedagogy for the arts and humanities. *Pedagogy, 6*(2), 261–287. https://doi.org/10.1215/15314200-2005-004

Ballengee-Morris, C. B. (2019). Cultural pluralism—Looking forward. In D. Garnet & A. Sinner (Eds.), *Art, culture, and pedagogy* (pp. 77–84). Brill.

Bell, L. (2010). *Storytelling for social justice: Connecting narrative and the arts in antiracist teaching.* Routledge. https://doi.org/10.4324/9781315101040

Bell, L. A., & Desai, D. (2011). Imagining otherwise: Connecting the arts and social justice to envision and act for change: Special issue introduction. *Equity & Excellence in Education, 44*(3), 287–295. https://doi.org/10.1080/10665684.2011.591672

Bertling, J. G. (2015). The art of empathy: A mixed methods case study of a critical place-based art education program. *International Journal of Education & the Arts, 16*(13). http://www.ijea.org/v16n13/

Bey, S. (2013). Excavating the cityscape through urban tales and local archives. *Art Education, 66*(4), 14–21. https://doi.org/10.1080/00043125.2013.11519227

Blandy, D. (2011). Sustainability, participatory culture, and the performance of democracy: Ascendant sites of theory and practice in art education. *Studies in Art Education, 52*(3), 243–255. https://doi.org/10.1080/00393541.2011.11518838

Blandy, D., & Hoffman, E. (1993). Toward an art education of place. *Studies in Art Education, 35*(1), 22–33. https://doi.org/10.2307/1320835

Bolin, P. E. (2020). Looking forward from where we have been. *Art Education, 73*(5), 44–46. https://doi.org/10.1080/00043125.2020.1766925

Boughton, D. (2004). Assessing art learning in changing contexts: High-stakes accountability, international standards and changing conceptions of artistic development. In E. W. Eisner & M. D. Day (Eds.), *Handbook of research and policy in art education* (pp. 585–605). Routledge.

Buffington, M. B. (2007). The service-learning and art education. *Art Education, 60*(6), 40–45. https://doi.org/10.1080/00043125.2007.11651132

Carpenter, B. S., & Tavin, K. M. (2010). Drawing (past, present, and future) together: A (graphic) look at the reconceptualization of art education. *Studies in Art Education, 51*(4), 327–352. https://doi.org/10.1080/00393541.2010.11518812

Childs, M. C. (2001). Civic ecosystems. *Journal of Urban Design, 6*(1), 55–72. https://doi.org/10.1080/13574800120032879

Clark, G., & Zimmerman, E. (2000). Greater understanding of the local community a community-based art education program for rural schools. *Art Education, 53*(2), 33–39. https://doi.org/10.2307/3193848

Coats, C. (2020). Embrace art education's indiscernibility. *Art Education, 73*(4), 44–47. https://doi.org/10.1080/00043125.2020.1717818

Desai, D. (2010). Reflections on social justice art teacher education. In T. Anderson, K. Khallmark, & D. Gussak (Eds.), *Art education for social justice* (pp. 172–178). National Art Education Association.

Dewey, J. (2011). *Democracy and education; An introduction to the philosophy of education.* Simon & Brown.

Dewhurst, M. (2010). An inevitable question: Exploring the defining features of social justice art education. *Art Education, 63*(5), 6–13. https://doi.org/10.1080/00043125.2010.11519082

Dewhurst, M. (2011). Where is the action? Three lenses to analyze social justice art education. *Equity & Excellence in Education, 44*(3), 364–378. https://doi.org/10.1080/10665684.2011.591261

Duncombe, S. (2016). Does it work? The effect of activist art. *Social Research: An International Quarterly, 83*(1), 115–134. https://doi.org/10.1353/sor.2016.0005

Duncum, P. (2018). Towards foundations for a socially critical art education (8th annual Leon Jackman memorial lecture). *Australian Art Education, 39*(1), 17–29.

Dyer, C. (2021). Critical pedagogy and visual culture art education in a cosplay-based curriculum. *Transformative Works and Cultures, 35.* https://doi.org/10.3983/twc.2021.1987

Eckhoff, A. (2011). Transformative partnerships: Designing school-based visual arts outreach programmes. *International Journal of Art & Design Education, 30*(2), 256–265. https://doi.org/10.1111/j.1476-8070.2011.01701.x

Eisner, E. W. (1972). *Educating artistic vision.* Macmillan.

Gaztambide-Fernandez, R. (2013). Why the arts don't "do" anything: Toward a new vision for cultural production in education. *Harvard Educational Review, 83*(1), 211–237. https://doi.org/10.17763/haer.83.1.a78q39699078ju20

Graham, M. (2007). Art, ecology and art education: Locating art education in a critical place-based pedagogy. *Studies in Art Education, 48*(4), 375–391. https://doi.org/10.1080/00393541.2007.11650115

Graham, M. (2019). Assessment in the visual arts: Challenges and possibilities. *Arts Education Policy Review, 120*(3), 175–183. https://doi.org/10.1080/1063 2913.2019.1579131

Gray, S. R., & Graham, M. A. (2007). This is the right place. *Journal of Museum Education, 32*(3), 301–310. https://doi.org/10.1080/10598650.2007.11510580

Greene, M. (1995). *Releasing the imagination: Essays on education, the arts, and social change.* Jossey-Bass Publishers. https://doi.org/10.1086/444145

Habib, S. (2019). Portraits of place: Critical pedagogy in the classroom. In *Identities, youth and belonging* (pp. 177–194). Springer. https://doi.org/10.1007/978-3-319-96113-2_11

Hutzel, K., Bastos, F. M. C., & Cosier, K. (2012). *Transforming city schools through art: Approaches to meaningful K-12 learning.* Teachers College Press. https://doi.org/10.5860/choice.50-0424

Hutzel, K., Russell, R., & Gross, J. (2010). Eighth-graders as role models: A service-learning art collaboration for social and emotional learning. *Art Education, 63*(4), 12–18. https://doi.org/10.1080/00043125.2010.11519074

Hyungsook, K. (2014). Socially engaged art practice and character education: Understanding others through visual art. *International Journal of Education Through Art, 10*(1), 55–69. https://doi.org/10.1386/eta.10.1.55_1

Inwood, H. J. (2008). At the crossroads: Situating place-based art education. *Canadian Journal of Environmental Education (CJEE), 13*(1), 29–41. https://openjournal.lakeheadu.ca/index.php/cjee/article/view/871

Kraehe, A. M. (2018). Arts equity. *Art Education, 71*(1), 4–6. https://doi.org/10.1080/00043125.2018.1389576

Kraehe, A. M. (2020). The future of art curriculum: Imagining and longing beyond "the now." *Art Education, 73*(3), 4–5. https://doi.org/10.1080/00043125.2020.1738843

Kraehe, A. M., & Acuff, J. B. (2013). Theoretical considerations for art education research with and about "underserved" populations. *Studies in Art Education, 54*(4), 294–309. https://doi.org/10.1080/00393541.2013.11518904

Lawton, P. H., Walker, M. A., & Green, M. (2019). *Community-based art education across the lifespan: Finding common ground.* Teachers College Press.

London, P. (1994). *Step outside: Community-based art education.* Heinemann.

López, V., Pereira, A., & Rao, S. S. (2017). Baltimore uprising: Empowering pedagogy for change. *Art Education, 70*(4), 33–37. https://doi.org/10.1080/00043125.2017.1317555

Mernick, A. (2021). Critical arts pedagogy: Nurturing critical consciousness and self-actualization through art education. *Art Education, 74*(5), 19–24. https://doi.org/10.1080/00043125.2021.1928468

Peppler, K., Dahn, M., & Ito, M. (2022). connected arts learning: Cultivating equity through connected and creative educational experiences. *Review of Research in Education, 46*(1), 264–287. https://doi.org/10.3102/0091732X221084322

Powell, K. A. (2008). ReMapping the City: Palimpset, place, and identity in art education research. *Studies in Art Education, 50*(1), 6–21. https://doi.org/10.1080/00393541.2008.11518752

Powell, K., & Lajevic, L. (2011). Emergent places in preservice art teaching: Lived curriculum, relationality, and embodied knowledge. *Studies in Art Education, 53*(1), 35–52.

Quinn, T. (2021). Out of cite, out of mind: Social justice and art education, 29(1), 1–5. https://doi.org/10.1080/03098260500030223

Quinn, T. M., Ploof, J., & Hochtritt, L. J. (2012). *Art and social justice education: Culture as commons*. Routledge. https://doi.org/10.4324/9780203852477

Rollins, T. (2019). How do you get to prospect avenue? In A. Wexler & V. Sabbaghi (Eds.), *Bridging communities through socially engaged art* (pp. 79–88). Springer. https://doi.org/10.4324/9781351175586-9

Schlemmer, R. H., Carpenter, B. S., & Hitchcock, E. (2017). Socially engaged art education: Practices, processes, and possibilities. *Art Education, 70*(4), 56–59. https://doi.org/10.1080/00043125.2017.1317564

Sobel, D. (1997) Sense of place education for the elementary years. In *Coming home: Developing a sense of place in our communities and schools. Proceedings of the 1997 forum*. ERIC Document: ED421312. https://files.eric.ed.gov/fulltext/ED421312.pdf

Stephens, P. G. (2006). A real community bridge: Informing community-based learning through a model of participatory public art. *Art Education, 59*(2), 40–46. https://doi.org/10.1080/00043125.2006.11651586

Stuhr, P., Ballengee-Morris, C., & Daniel, V. A. H. (2008). Social justice through curriculum: Investigating issues of diversity. In R. Mason & T. Esca (Eds.), *International dialogues in art education* (pp. 81–95). Intellect Books.

Taylor, P. G., Carpenter, B. S., Ballengee-Morris, C., & Sessions, B. (2006). *Interdisciplinary approaches to teaching art in high school*. National Art Education Association.

Trafí-Prats, L. (2012). Urban children and intellectual emancipation: Video narratives of self and place in the city of Milwaukee. *Studies in Art Education, 53*(2), 125–138. https://doi.org/10.1080/00393541.2012.11518857

Ulbricht, J. (2005). *What is community-based art education?* Taylor & Francis. https://doi.org/10.1080/00043125.2005.11651529

Vinnakota, R. (2019). *From civic education to a civic learning ecosystem: A landscape analysis and case for collaboration* [Research Report]. Red and Blue Works. https://rbw.civic-learning.org/wp-content/uploads/2019/12/CE_online.pdf

Wagaman, M. A. (2011). Social empathy as a framework for adolescent empowerment. *Journal of Social Service Research, 37*(3), 278–293. https://doi.org/10.1080/01488376.2011.564045

Zembylas, M. (2018). Reinventing critical pedagogy as decolonizing pedagogy: The education of empathy. *Review of Education, Pedagogy, and Cultural Studies, 40*(5), 404–421. https://doi.org/10.1080/10714413.2019.1570794

Section II
Think

3 Positioning Students as Arts-Based Researchers

Building out of the concepts in the previous section, we begin Section II by exploring the role of students in the learning process. By positioning teens as arts-based researchers, we adopt a student-centered approach to curriculum design, asking students to identify and utilize their strengths as they move through locally bound and personally relevant learning experiences (Shields et al., 2020). As we consider the centrality of positioning students as independent researchers, we will revisit the importance of the arts in helping students develop a research process. The emphasis on students as arts-based researchers is foundational to our curriculum proposal and revisits key ideas from Section I, where envisioning students as arts-based researchers aligns with our vision of students as empowered and creative civic agents. The chapter will review how artmaking as a process of researching, developed through material reflection and engagement (i.e., learning about people, visiting places, and researching events), opens up possibilities for students to make artwork that interprets and applies their understanding (of history, politics, social issues, etc.) to a contemporary, local context. Through this act of filtering research on larger issues through the lens of the local, civic learning is embedded as students seek to understand their immediate community, make artwork that processes this thinking, and design future action pointing toward progress and change. This chapter establishes how positioning students as arts-based researchers is at the core of a civically engaged art curriculum by introducing our pedagogical framework of think | make | act. These three concepts will be revisited again in Chapter 4 as we present the pedagogical tools we used in our own work with young people.

In this chapter, we present a macro view of each of our spiraling think | make | act components. In Chapter 2 we presented an overview of art education trends, highlighting how art classrooms can be school-centered, locally bound, historically relevant, inherently critical, and future-oriented. This pedagogical framing is necessary to activate the three-dimensional civic model introduced in Chapter 1. It is not possible to envision an art

DOI: 10.4324/9781003199106-5

classroom as a space that builds civic capacities through the development of civic knowledge, skills and dispositions, without art classrooms becoming places for more than just artmaking. Thusly, Chapter 1 put forward the notion that processes of cultural production do the work of activating civic knowledge, skills, and dispositions, and that young people are interested in this kind of work; and concludes that it is necessary to present an expansive understanding of artistic behaviors by adding the necessity for explicitly teaching students how artists engage civic spaces. In this second section of the volume, we bring our empirical, theoretical, and pedagogical framing together to conceptualize a curriculum that invites students to think, make, and act as local arts-based researchers.

Think | make | act

Think | make | act has become the rough framework for the building blocks of our civically engaged art education curriculum (See: Fig. 3.1). These three actions have become our shorthand reference to the way we interpret the civic capacities from the C3 Framework explored in Section I (knowledge, skills, and values) through processes of artmaking, allowing art to serve as the keystone component to civic engagement. The think | make | act model is an iterative cycle that can be spiraled over and over again in the art classroom. The notion of spiral design is not a new one, with Bruner (1960) first introducing the concept. Traditional conceptions of curriculum relate to how teaching and learning happens in a linear fashion; however, when considering teaching and learning spiraling from the act of creating through art, we must also consider how things may emerge, pushing the curriculum outside of linear understandings. This alternate formation of knowledge allows for teaching and learning to contextualize each other and provides a way of knowing through action and reflection, as the teacher and students spiral through learning together. At the core then, a spiraling curriculum should be one that is cyclical, meaning

THINK.
Intersect social justice + subjectivity

MAKE.
Transform art practice into praxis

ACT.
Build community

Figure 3.1 Think | make | act diagram

students should return to and revisit a topic multiple times in school; the topic should have increasing depth and invite students to engage in thinking at more complex levels with each iteration; and finally, spiraling curriculum should move out of prior knowledge by asking students to connect and expand on the foundational models of the subject presented in earlier spirals. For us, the concept of curriculum as spiraling means that art as a civic pursuit can be introduced to kids of any age, with the teacher attending to the scaffolding and focus at each level.

When beginning to spiral through a curricular model that holds both civics and art as central components, we believe that a place-based approach is a generative starting point. In an educational climate where 21st-century skills are marketed as moving students toward global citizenship, we argue that before young people have the capacity to be global citizens, they must first learn to be citizens of their local communities. When students are taught to engage and care for the communities they come from, schooling has the potential to become a transformative local project aimed at producing engaged citizens who might later participate at a state, national, or global level. Teaching toward this kind of sustained civic engagement should not be confused with service learning or community service, which are quickly finding their way into secondary schools, as universities incorporate service hour requirements into admission portfolios. This model of engagement results in some young people doing projects in their communities to receive hours, not because they are invested in the community itself (this model aligns with the personally responsible citizenship model, discussed in Chapter 1). The resulting levels of engagement are not sustainable and may foster counterproductive outcomes like a lack of motivation to continue volunteering and ultimately contribute to a decrease in civic attitudes and behaviors (Gallant et al., 2010). Essentially, this mode of civic engagement is focused on checking a local participation box with the goal of ultimately leaving that community behind to pursue higher education. This reinforces the idea that engagement in communities is only a requisite for leaving those communities in pursuit of some sort of upward advancement (Ball & Lai, 2006). This then extends into experiences in higher education, where colleges and universities claim to serve the communities they are situated in by incorporating service learning projects and requirements, but in reality, are using these community projects to prepare students to leave in search of the next opportunity; quickly becoming a cycle continuing outward and further divorcing young people from a physical place to both claim and care for. This model of learning in communities breeds a type of service tourism, where places serve the people living in them, instead of people serving the places they live in, breeding a model of civic engagement that positions the community as a resource to be used up, but not replenished or invested in (Ball & Lai, 2006).

While the empirical support for these types of mandatory service learning experiences in secondary and undergraduate programs remains unclear, research does indicate "that it is the nature of students' experiences, not merely their participation in community service, which leads to ongoing civic engagement" (Gallant et al., 2010, p. 197). This work proposes that if you are going to include service learning or community service experiences, then schools and teachers should work to make these experiences meaningful beyond just their requirement in the curriculum. Suggesting that creating opportunities for students to find and make meaning inside of the community is critical for that experience to prompt further engagement. This shift opens up potential for our think | make | act curricular spiral where communities are sites of learning, where teachers and students view the community and its resources as materials for research, and where student-led research drives further community investment (Desai, 2002; Ulbricht, 2005). In the section that follows, we argue that students must *think* as local researchers, and *make* as contemporary artists, to be able to move toward *acting* as engaged community members.

Thinking like historians

To be able to begin to spiral through think | make | act, it is important for teachers to make decisions about what will be the starting point for student inquiry. We suggest the opportunity to learn about local histories offers an emerging site of inquiry that connects students to one another, their community, and broader national dialogues. This type of place-based pedagogy posits that places, specifically local places, hold potential to support a curriculum that is meaningful, relevant, and accessible for young people. While we reviewed place-based approaches to art education in Chapter 2, here we want to highlight the relevance of local places as the bigger educational goal of teaching toward civic engagement. Place-based education is a pedagogical framework that positions learning inside of local communities, cultures, experiences, and people. This model uses local places as a point of entry for students to learn about a range of subjects, and for us, this learning happens through history, civics, and art. Proponents of place-based pedagogies believe that "connecting projects to community, delving into authentic problems, and encouraging public products develop an ethic of contribution" (Vander Ark et al., 2020, p. 2). This ethics of contribution is akin to our earlier discussion of civic engagement as utilizing civic knowledge, skills, and dispositions to begin to identify, understand, and impact the community.

Art education conversations around "sense of place" have been happening for decades (Anderson & Milbrandt, 1998, 2005). Although, in our practice as in-service and pre-service educators we have found that the concept of place often manifests in predictable ways, with curriculum focused on essential questions like: Who are you? What places do you feel connected to? While these essential questions start teachers on the path to student-centered curricula, they are rarely supported by curriculum materials that ask P-12 students to think deeply by engaging in research about the communities they live in. This is where we believe civically engaged art education can expand and contribute to the conversation surrounding civic engagement in schools. To begin to experience civic engagement, young people must have opportunities to become familiar with meaningful participation within communities, where they may experience outward impact and outcomes (Flanagan, 2004). These concepts might be expanded more when viewed alongside research linking how people's attachment to place results in their commitment to those places (Stefaniak et al., 2017). At the core of these meaningful, local, inquiry experiences lies the theory of place attachment. This theory posits that despite increased globalization and mobility, place is still important to people, and local communities, in particular cities and homes, hold the most meaningful points of attachment for people. Interestingly, the neighborhood, the area between the city and the home, is a location that people report significantly lower attachment. More disheartening is that when neighborhoods are socially and ethnically diverse, there is even less attachment reported (Lewicka, 2011). We imagine this trend will continue as the number of school choice districts and charter schools continue to climb. So, as schooling becomes increasingly decentralized and the neighborhood school model disappears, we see a connection between individuals' investment in neighborhoods and the shifting role of schools within communities.

The National Center for Educational Statistics (2019) reported that between fall 2009 and fall 2019, public charter school enrollment more than doubled, and this does not take into account the increases in charter school attendance in a post-pandemic world. Adding to this is the growing number of districts allowing for school choice. In 2016, the National Center for Educational Statistics reported that 41% of families indicated that public school choice was available (Wang et al., 2019). While this is not a critique of charter schooling or school choice, the fact remains that these systems contribute to the disappearance of the neighborhood school. These are the "unintended consequences of what market-driven school reform" has done to the landscape of public schools, which also likely impacts the ways that individuals are attached to their immediate communities or neighborhoods (McWilliams, 2019, p. 15). Amidst all this there is a silver lining, place attachment demonstrates that the strength of community connections is perhaps the strongest indicator of attachment (Lewicka, 2011). So if strength of connections positively impacts attachment, and attachment then impacts engagement, perhaps learning about local communities and neighborhoods becomes a way for young people to begin to forge attachments to the places they live.

While research into place attachment spans a diverse range of academic fields, relatively little has connected attachment to local places with civic engagement in young people, with a few notable exceptions where researchers found a connection between researching local histories, development of place attachment, and an enhanced sense of community pride and civic engagement (Pearson & Plevyak, 2020; Stefaniak et al., 2017). When viewed together, you start to see why a curriculum spiral that begins with an investigation of local places, neighborhoods, and communities might be an important starting point for young people. This project uses this emerging research to establish our interest in local community histories, and uses community histories as a springboard for making art and later acting as engaged citizens. But before students can make and act, they must think. For us, historians are doing the kinds of thinking that are critical to beginning projects based in local community histories. The field of social studies education offers a wealth of knowledge surrounding the practice of doing history with young people and in this, we find approaches to teaching students to think like local historians.

> "Doing history" conveys how we prefer to use history as a term that names an activity or set of practices. History for us is something that people can choose to do, to create, to write, to produce, to perform, and to imagine.
>
> (Donnelly & Norton, 2020, p. 4)

At its core, the concept of *doing history* is a reconceptualization of what history is and does. In short, the field of history has drawn into question whether objects and artifacts of the past can be separated from interpretation. The notion that reality, and thus history, cannot be accurately captured through the language of interpretation is central to the notion of doing history. Because history is studied in the present, and the present is separated from the past, there is no way of knowing if the version of history being interpreted is the reality of the past. Instead, it is just that, an interpretation of a collection of objects, stories, images, and documents that are strung together to create a speculation of history. This means that the same history can be done differently by different people, for different reasons, and with different outcomes (Donnelly & Norton, 2020).

Doing history in local communities challenges educators to adopt the methods historians use to facilitate student learning about local history. To do local history, students must think like historians, using source material to create their own knowledge, instead of simply reading or studying the history compiled in a textbook. As students act as historical researchers, they are looking back and gazing forward, doing the important work of situating local narratives inside state and national histories. This creates an opportunity to see how history happened in the community, and how their local streets, graveyards, churches, libraries, and other institutions hold a more personal and accessible view of broader historical moments. This model of education is generative, holding onto the pedagogical hope that in learning about the past, young people might become better stewards of the present. The practice of doing history provides approaches to historical learning that might later open up opportunities for civic action. Asking young people to position histories in the present, to unpack how social and political forces shaped local history, and how the ripples of history extend into the present.

Through thinking like historians, young people learn about the history of their communities and to see how their communities were built and grew. They also learn how their community histories fit into a broader social, national, or global moment. As students access archival material, listen to oral histories, visit local sites, and do the work that historians do, they are being asked to research the past and filter that material through themselves. But is learning about local histories enough?

In fact, there is a long tradition of thought that regards the study of history as being at best a waste of time and at worst potentially harmful. An interesting entry point into this line of thinking is Hayden White's essay "The Burden of History" (1966). White argued here that history failed to match either the predictive value of science or the imaginative power of art.

(Donnelly & Norton, 2020, p. 9)

Making like artists

We, like White (1966), see the imaginative power of the arts as critical to activating young people's understanding of local histories. Instead of making art about history, we wonder how the arts offer opportunities for making with local histories. This place-driven approach to teaching and learning holds close parallels to the models of art education reviewed in Chapter 2. It is using these through lines from the world of art education that we can suggest how art classrooms become a site for thinking civics differently. We have seen how social studies education offers a productive model for doing historical thinking and learning; in particular, the ways that social studies education takes up the local landscape as sites for doing history. Now we move to envision what artistic engagement with the materials of these places offers, and how that might continue our curriculum spiral by moving students toward action. This allows the art teacher to begin to conceive of how they might facilitate students making art with the places they live in. While making art is often what art education is associated with, we believe in a version of art education that is grounded in thinking like an artist; without this model of thinking as an artistic researcher, artmaking becomes more about making projects, than making research. So, what does making look like when it is grounded in the practice of research?

When thinking of artmaking as a research practice, we looked to scholars in the world of arts-based research to inform our understanding. Within this, the work of Sullivan (2006; 2010) resonates with possibilities for reimagining what the art classroom might look like. When positioning students as arts-based researchers, the art teacher must remember the final work of art does not determine the depth or breadth of the student's investigation, but rather the work of making art highlights an arc of learning and transformation. Art teachers, along with their students, must engage in a complex web of activity that investigates ideas over time and through various means and materials. Sullivan (2006) calls this the "*practice* of creative artworks, and the processes, products, proclivities, and contexts that support this activity" (p. 26). Thus, a focus on theories of production becomes the central concern for the art teacher. The practice of making art as an act of research is underlined by a conceptualization of artist practice that moves beyond knowing, toward artistic investigations that further understanding and meaning making. This shift indicates a fundamental reconfiguration of the art classroom. Instead of asking what students know about art and artmaking, we might instead ask questions about how students are making meaning through artmaking (Bruner, 1996; Sullivan, 2010).

> Any worthwhile art education proposal must be based on how artists think and what they do... Artists' distinctive quality of mind is that *they see for themselves.* Their whole stance to life, what fuels their creativity, is their insistence upon engaging with life directly and making up their own minds about what is of value and what needs improvement. Like scientists and intellectually courageous people in any discipline, artists require direct access to the world, secondhand sources are inadequate. They need to encounter the raw material. Through this unmitigated contact with the world, artists enjoy the pleasure of witnessing the world as if for the first time.
>
> (London, 1994, pp. 28–29)

Art teachers must be well versed in how artists work, they must look at contemporary art with their students, grapple with artistic process, and experiment with mediums, as they overlay the historical framing from their early, archival and historical research experiences with the process of making art. This making is not divorced from the thinking in the earlier spiral, but rather an extension of students' thinking about local histories. Through these explorations, students should engage in a range of material practices, allowing them to expand and develop their visual repertoire. Art materials become a mode of inquiry and their qualities or material traits become ripe with possibilities for developing understanding. Perhaps more important is that art teachers' understanding of what the materials of artmaking are must expand. Meaning the materials of their historical research become artistic materials in their investigations; for example, sound recordings, photographs, or rubbings from a site visit may be as useful a material as paint or clay. By expanding the materials of making to include more than just art supplies, students widen their repertoire of tools to understand and communicate.

But access to materials is not the only requisite component of these making experiences, instead students must use materials in ways that draw out meaning. Rather than the teacher giving a demonstration on how to use an oil pastel, the teacher might instead engage students in a focused exploration of oil pastels while guiding a discussion on what makes the oil pastel a unique material. To borrow from Ingold (2007), what is the oiliness or pasteliness and what do these qualities allow you to do, say, or think? In this way, the first sweep of the pastel may not carry meaning, but when that pastel is laid over an archival photograph or scratched through to reveal something underneath, knowledge begins to unfold. By guiding students toward an understanding of artmaking as a layered, complex, never-ending process, we start to highlight how the student is a researcher, artist, and thinker.

This model of teaching and learning draws upon contemporary artists, materials, and practices, after all, "[a]rtists have been visionaries for centuries—why are we not aligning with the visionaries rather than the regulators?" (Coats, 2020, p. 46). This complex process of making does not come easy, instead, it requires that both the art teacher and student rethink what learning is, what art classrooms are for, and finally, what their respective roles in these processes are. Aoki conceptualizes this as a moment of living within the tension of curriculum as planned and curriculum as lived and "calls on us pedagogues to make time for meaningful striving and struggling, time for letting things be, time for question, time for singing, time for crying, time for anger, time for praying and hoping" (Aoki et al., 2004, p. 164). This element of time is critical for developing ideas, [re]forming notions of self, and for doing the complex work of creative thinking and critical problem solving.

Positioning students as arts-based researchers is useful for introducing the work of making art, without overlooking the qualities embedded in art practice. It "transforms our identities and gives new ways of expressing our differently evolving identities" (Finley, 2014, p. 531). What Finley (2011, 2014) proposed, and what we find important in this mode of working with students, is an allowance for coming into knowledge during the artmaking process. This open-ended, insightful, and generative exploration is centered on student interest and investment in learning about their community, as students filter their learning through the artmaking process. Positioning students as arts-based researchers has deep resonance and impact in an educational landscape that is often focused on individual accomplishment over collective learning. This kind of work in the art classroom offers opportunities for the arts to do what they do best, discover and invent a more hopeful world (Finley, 2008, 2011, 2018). Arts-based practices give students the opportunity to investigate their social, political, and cultural worlds and through the outcomes of their making, opens up opportunities for others to see, feel, and experience them. Positioning students as arts-based researchers might then be viewed as an emancipatory project, shifting the location of research, and for us, learning, into the "places where people meet" (Finley, 2008, p. 74).

Acting as a community member

Positioning students as arts-based researchers stretches engagement beyond making art and engaging in artistic behaviors. It means that young people need to do the kind of deep community connecting that artists do. We need students to think like artists, like community members, like civic participants. We, along with others, believe that schools are not offering opportunities for this kind of critical engagement with the social and political worlds kids live in, so the art classroom must find ways to scaffold more than just artmaking. We have begun to wonder what happens when students think not just like artists, but also as public historians; this viewpoint challenges "assumptions about what art education should do or look like: Namely, art education creates objects, the teacher is the authority who knows in advance what will be produced, and the classroom is structured around students working individually" (Coats, 2020, p. 45).

What if within the space of the art classroom, teachers facilitated the development of meaningful connections to the community through critical, artistic investigations of local histories? London (1994) argued for a view of art education that holds children's interests and experiences as central and relevant. Instead of asking young people to engage in an exploration of a predetermined lesson or objective, he presented a view of art education that positioned the community as the resource for idea generation. This process is likened to the work of artists and creatives, in that they are experiencing their direct world and wrestling with their understanding through the creation of artwork.

Where our work departs from this view of art education is in the outcomes. The aims of a civically engaged art curriculum stretch beyond the creation of an art object to include outcomes that focus on civic capacities, or the application of civic knowledge, skills, and values. These processes are inherently both student and community-centered. This means expanding a definition of art outcomes to include things like fostering a sense of belonging in a community (Desai, 2019). This model is further expanded on in social studies education where a model of action civics exists. "Through this model students *do* civics and *behave as citizens* by engaging in a cycle of research, action, and reflection upon problems they care about personally" (Levinson, 2015, p. 189). Within this spiral of action civics, the first cycle of engagement hinges on examining the community. It is in these early stages of doing civics that students must find an entry point into their communities, and for our projects, local histories have become a deep well of opportunity.

As they move through research into communities, they use critical art-making practices to render communities visible and begin to develop the dispositions necessary to devise and implement strategies for action. It is through thinking like historians and making like contemporary artists, they begin to focus their work on some aspect of their local history that connects back to their own experiences and realities. Reminding us that "people who don't enter history—that is people who do not appear in texts—are not studied ... [thus] the penalty of invisibility is that there is no source or repository of pride in accomplishment" (Ellison, 1952; London, 1994, p. 44). The types of arts-based research practices we present in this book have an interest in remaking local communities and of rendering the invisible, visible (Barone & Eisner, 2011; Ellison, 1952). As young people learn about their communities, they also render themselves as visible local participants. By acknowledging the value of their viewpoints, their interests, and their communities, the art classroom might become a place for curricular outcomes that encourage and celebrate this visibility and share it outward. Students may see themselves in historical people, or connect to a historic place because of its connection to their own personal cartography, or even see themselves in historic events as they watch them play out again in the present. Whatever the connection, these threads create opportunities for young people to become part of their communities, reiterating that a connection to civic spaces is at the heart of civic engagement. To begin to experience this connection, young people must have opportunities to become familiar with meaningful participation within local communities, where they may experience activities that impact communal outcomes (Flanagan, 2004).

According to Flanagan and Faison (2001), to develop competencies in civic engagement, young people need civic skills, or the ability to assist a community in furthering its objectives, and civic attachment, or a sense that their own, individual actions can make a difference. This project's short-term goals are to provide an opportunity for teens to become aware of the rich history of their community and begin to use artmaking to work through how they might use this history to inform future action. Sullivan (2006) reminds us that these are transformative acts and "if the purpose of research is the creation of new knowledge, then the outcome is not merely to help explain things…but to fully understand them in a way that helps us act on that knowledge" (p. 22). If the local community and its history is being researched, and students are beginning to render themselves visible in that history, how might these practices open up possibilities for action?

To begin to spiral through action in this think | make | act model, we must highlight the legitimacy of acting as a community member as a prerequisite for civic engagement. Like any community-driven curricular project, the ability to act in the community must be facilitated by students, and students are not able to act in their communities if they do not identify as community members. Through learning about local histories, developing an attachment to local places, then creating artwork connecting to local places and histories, students begin to see themselves as part of their communities, and have "an increased willingness to become civically engaged" (Stefaniak et al., 2017, para. 3). Our aim in the act spiral is for students to encounter the historical significance of communities, while also providing tools and strategies for students and teachers to engage fully in their communities. This kind of collective learning opportunity is a unique occasion to discover and integrate concepts, perspectives, and best practices from both history and the arts to craft generative and authentic encounters for students to write, draw, paint, or make themselves into their communities.

In this work, artmaking becomes a space for students to develop critical ideas, agency, and a sense of authorship. In this way, the process of making art is more than a mode of expression; instead, artmaking and the artwork produced become spaces for reflexive thinking and processing. This work suggests that artmaking is an invitation to do research, gather information, and articulate informed perspectives. This situates art as providing young people ways to contribute to dialogues around civics in their local communities, allowing them to envision themselves as capable of making an impact and being heard. Suggesting that as teens develop an understanding of society and what it means to be a citizen from everyday encounters, they continue the earlier spirals of thinking and making (Clay & Rubin, 2020). This sense of community is one of particular interest, because when we are deeply connected with where we come from, it is difficult to draw a line between individual identities and the communities that shape them (Cahill et al., 2008). For young people, these encounters influence how citizenship is interpreted and later enacted.

Ultimately, this final component of action might be interpreted in vastly different ways depending on the location in the larger spiral, but we suggest a connecting thread across all interpretations is the development and use of student voice. The concept of student voice can mean that students are able to identify problems, articulate opinions, or even suggest possible outcomes or solutions (Mitra, 2018). Mitra and Gross (2009) offer up the visual of a pyramid of student voice, with listening at the bottom, topped by collaboration, and leadership at the pyramid's pinnacle. As students move through these levels, they often move from independent work, to more collaborative projects, finally to projects that position them as community leaders, a moment where students possess the most agency (Mitra, 2018). What we propose in this final section of our think | make | act framework is that action does not have to begin with changing the community, instead teachers and students must realize this work is iterative and builds slowly. Through researching and thinking and making art about and with local places, students are beginning to see themselves as part of those places as they work toward an inclusive, collective community memory. Through their historical research and artmaking, students engage in an exploration of the ways that history both endures through time and is also modified, erased, or buried. The fragile and malleable character of history is a reminder that it is always, in some ways, a reflection of the present. As students investigate what sparked their interest from the past, they hone in on what begs for more attention, identifying what part of the community they belong to and how it needs them in it. Then they begin these investigations again, doing the work that the *action civics* model puts forward, where "students *do* civics and *behave as citizens* by engaging in a cycle of research, action, and reflection upon problems they care about personally" (Levinson, 2015, p. 189). The stages of these programs are (Levinson, 2015, p. 190):

1 Examine your community
2 Choose an issue
3 Research the issue and set a goal
4 Analyze power
5 Develop strategies
6 Take action and affect policy

While students might need to cycle through the first 3 or 4 phases multiple times before they are able to begin to develop strategies and take action, these earlier stages of action civics are still action oriented as they are doing the work of acting as community members. They are investigating, researching, and creating about their communities, they are developing a sense of belonging to these communities, they are learning about the past and present of their communities, and one day they will be able to take the kinds of action that impact the future of their communities.

Conclusion

The next two chapters of this section take you into the think | make | act model and invite you to see how we chose to investigate and explore our local community with a group of teens. The chapters guide you through the curricular strategies we enacted in our project with local teens in a summer program investigating the history of the civil rights movement in Tallahassee, Florida. Here, we give you a detailed overview of the specific teaching and learning strategies we developed and implemented in our own community investigation. Then, in Section III, we offer individual illustrative cases highlighting students from our summer program. Here we include images, quotes, and reflections illustrating how these young people engaged in the deeply personal work of researching community history through site visits, interviews, and artmaking. These chapters are meant to be examples of how this kind of curricular project might look in action and give you inspiration and motivation for designing something similar for your own classrooms, summer camps, or after-school programs.

References

Anderson, T., & Milbrandt, M. (1998). Authentic instruction in art: Why and how to dump the school art style. *Visual Arts Research*, 24(1), 13–20.

Anderson, T., & Milbrandt, M. (2005). *Art for life: Authentic instruction in art.* McGraw-Hill.

Aoki, T. T., Pinar, W. F., & Irwin, R. L. (2004). *Curriculum in a new key: The collected works of Ted t. Aoki.* Routledge. https://doi.org/10.4324/9781410611390

Ball, E. L., & Lai, A. (2006). Place-based pedagogy for the arts and humanities. *Pedagogy*, 6(2), 261–287. https://doi.org/10.1215/15314200-2005-004

Barone, T., & Eisner, E. W. (2011). *Arts based research*. Sage. https://doi.org/10.4135/9781452230627

Bruner, J. (1960). *Process of education*. Harvard University Press. https://doi.org/10.1002/bs.3830090108

Bruner, J. (1996). *The culture of education*. Harvard University Press. https://doi.org/10.4159/9780674251083

Cahill, C., Rios-Moore, I., & Threatts, T. (2008). Different eyes/open eyes: Community-based participatory action research. In J. Cammarota & M. Fine (Eds.), *Revolutionizing education: Youth participatory action research in motion* (pp. 89–124). Routledge. https://doi.org/10.5130/ijcre.v3i0.1157

Clay, K. L., & Rubin, B. C. (2020). "I look deep into this stuff because it's a part of me": Toward a critically relevant civics education. *Theory & Research in Social Education*, 48(2), 161–181. https://doi.org/10.1080/00933104.2019.1680466

Coats, C. (2020). Embrace art education's indiscernibility. *Art Education, 73*(4), 44–47. https://doi.org/10.1080/00043125.2020.1717818

Desai, D. (2002). The ethnographic move in contemporary art: What does it mean for art education? *Studies in Art Education, 43*(4), 307–323. https://doi.org/10.2307/1320980

Desai, D. (2019). Cultural diversity in art education. In K. Freedman (Ed.), *International encyclopedia for art and design education* (pp. 1–21). Wiley-Blackburn Publication. https://doi.org/10.1002/9781118978061.ead088

Donnelly, M., & Norton, C. (2020). *Doing history*. Routledge. https://doi.org/10.4324/9781003107781

Ellison, R. (1952). *Invisible man*. Random House.

Finley, S. (2008). Arts-based research. In J.G. Knowles & A.L. Cole (Eds.), *Handbook of the arts in qualitative research* (pp. 71–81). SAGE Publications. https://doi.org/10.4135/9781452226545.n6

Finley, S. (2011). Critical arts-based inquiry: The pedagogy and performance of a radical ethical aesthetic. In N. Denzin & Y. Lincoln (Eds.), *The SAGE handbook of qualitative research* (pp. 435–450; (4th ed.). Sage Handbook of Qualitative Research.

Finley, S. (2014). An introduction to critical arts-based research: Demonstrating methodologies and practices of a radical ethical aesthetic. *Cultural Studies? Critical Methodologies, 14*(6), 531–532. https://doi.org/10.1177/1532708614548123

Finley, S. (2018). The future of critical arts-based research: Creating aesthetic spaces for resistance politics. In *Qualitative inquiry in the public sphere* (pp. 194–207). Routledge. https://doi.org/10.4324/9781315143385-22

Flanagan, C. A. (2004). Volunteerism, leadership, political socialization, and civic engagement. In R. M. Lerner & L. Steinberg (Eds.), *Handbook of adolescent psychology* (pp. 721–745). John Wiley & Sons. https://doi.org/10.1002/9780471726746.ch23

Flanagan, C. A., & Faison, N. (2001). Youth civic development: Implications of research for social policy and programs. *Social Policy Report, 15*(1), 3–15.

Gallant, K., Smale, B., & Arai, S. (2010). Civic engagement through mandatory community service: Implications of serious leisure. *Journal of Leisure Research, 42*(2), 181–201. https://doi.org/10.1080/00222216.2010.11950201

Ingold, T. (2007). Materials against materiality. *Archaeological Dialogues, 14*(1), 1–16. https://doi.org/10.1017/s1380203807002127

Levinson, M. (2015). Action civics in the classroom. In *Social studies today* (pp. 189–197). Routledge. https://doi.org/10.4324/9781315726885-29

Lewicka, M. (2011). Place attachment: How far have we come in the last 40 years? *Journal of Environmental Psychology, 31*(3), 207–230. https://doi.org/10.1016/j.jenvp.2010.10.001

London, P. (1994). *Step outside: Community-based art education*. Heinemann.

McWilliams, J. A. (2019). *Compete or close: Traditional neighborhood schools under pressure*. Harvard Education Press.

Mitra, D. (2018). Student voice in secondary schools: The possibility for deeper change. *Journal of Educational Administration, 56*(5), 473–487. https://doi.org/10.1108/jea-01-2018-0007

Mitra, D. L., & Gross, S. J. (2009). Increasing student voice in high school reform: Building partnerships, improving outcomes. *Educational Management Administration & Leadership, 37*(4), 522–543. https://doi.org/10.1177/1741143209334577

National Center for Educational Statistics. (2019). *Charter schools.* Fast Facts. https://nces.ed.gov/fastfacts/display.asp?id=30

Pearson, A., & Plevyak, L. (2020). The effects of local history inquiry on community pride and civic engagement. *Citizenship Teaching & Learning, 15*(2), 135–153. https://doi.org/10.1386/ctl_00026_1

Shields, S. S., Fendler, R., & Henn, D. (2020). A vision of civically engaged art education: Teens as arts-based researchers. *Studies in Art Education, 61*(2), 123–141. https://doi.org/10.1080/00393541.2020.1740146

Stefaniak, A., Bilewicz, M., & Lewicka, M. (2017). The merits of teaching local history: Increased place attachment enhances civic engagement and social trust. *Journal of Environmental Psychology, 51,* 217–225. https://doi.org/10.1016/j.jenvp.2017.03.014

Sullivan, G. (2006). Research acts in art practice. *Studies in Art Education, 48*(1), 19–35. https://doi.org/10.1080/00393541.2006.11650497

Sullivan, G. (2010). *Art practice as research: Inquiry in visual arts.* Sage. https://doi.org/10.5860/choice.42-5662

Ulbricht, J. (2005). What is community-based art education? *Art Education, 58*(2), 6–12. https://doi.org/10.1080/00043125.2005.11651529

Vander Ark, T., Liebtag, E., & McClennen, N. (2020). *The power of place: Authentic learning through place-based education.* Association for Supervision & Curriculum Development.

Wang, K., Rathbun, A., & Musu, L. (2019). *School choice in the United States: 2019.* U.S. Department of Education. https://nces.ed.gov/pubs2019/2019106.pdf

White, H. V. (1966). The burden of history. *History and Theory, 5*(2), 111–134. https://doi.org/10.2307/2504510

4 Envisioning Curriculum

In this chapter, we spend time unpacking how positioning students as arts-based researchers in an art classroom gives them space to deeply engage in explorations of local people, places, and events. By viewing artmaking as a research process and the art classroom and local community as the location of these processes, this chapter provides a clear description of the ways that primary sources—like people, places, and events—can become a catalyst for student-driven inquiry into local communities. This chapter is in dialogue with Chapter 3, by offering a view of what centering people, places, and events looks like through pedagogical practice of think | make | act. Through this discussion, we give a broad overview of our project and situate our pedagogical decisions through the lens of our think | make | act curriculum spiral, introduced in Chapter 3. Then, Chapter 5 offers the reader an overview of the daily structure of our project, sharing tangible activities, questions, and strategies we implemented in our own work with teens. Chapters 4 and 5 are meant to complement one another, with Chapter 4 giving a macro view of pedagogical choices and Chapter 5 offering a micro view of curricular design.

Overview

> Ava: A lot of people understand the surface things. We've been taught, you know, about the civil rights movement over and over again since we were, like, in elementary school. But, you know, people don't *really* understand, like: oh, they did that, because they were *tired* of it. A lot of people don't really understand how *hard,* hard is.

In the summers of 2018 and 2019, we along with several graduate students, offered a week-long intensive art program to upper-middle and high school students focused on studying and reflecting on the legacy of the civil rights movement in Tallahassee, Florida. This program, titled the Tallahassee Foot Soldiers, carried the sub-title Change Makers Then and Now,

DOI: 10.4324/9781003199106-6

indicating our interest in approaching a project on the civil rights movement through the possibilities for youth civic action in the present. The program prioritized student-led research and engagement with primary source material, offering an experience where students spoke with activists and artists (people), explored the city (places), visited archives (events), and synthesized their experience through artmaking. The project targeted youth from local middle and high schools to engage in a participatory, arts-based project that facilitated youth inquiry into sites important to the legacy of the civil rights movement in Tallahassee, Florida. As the teens explored the heritage, history, and current issues important to their community, they produced artistic and didactic material that served to inform the development of curricular strategies for secondary teachers interested in working with their own local histories. The project looked at how young people engaged with the topic of civil rights, made connections to current events and issues, and developed engaged responses through artmaking. The inquiry was guided by two overarching questions: 1) How do arts practices provide an opening for youth to engage in critical questions concerning the local community? 2) What does positioning teens as arts-based researchers do to shape a civically engaged art education curriculum?

Methodology

For this project, we found ourselves with two separate research foci. The first positioned teens as arts-based researchers, and the second looked at how the practice of positioning students as arts-based researchers might inform a civically engaged art education curriculum. This type of nested inquiry is common when a project consists of two factors nested together (Peng, 2004). While nested inquiry is frequently used in mixed-method approaches to research, this format helped us conceptualize the dual foci of our own project. Our interest in both students as researchers and how their research practice informs curricular design is impossible to tease apart, as they are connected through the participation of the students. This was critical as we looked at the ways the teens engaged in thinking and making art with local histories, and how that might inform an art curriculum focused on civic engagement in local communities. As such, the teens were active participants in both phases of this participatory action research project (PAR). PAR, as it relates to educational research and curriculum development, is informed by critical pedagogy and emerged out of the field of adult education. PAR is influenced by Friere (1970) and assumes:

> The silenced are not just incidental to the curiosity of the researcher
> but are the masters of inquiry into the underlying causes of the events

in their world. In this context, research becomes a means of moving them beyond silence into a quest to proclaim the world.

(Freire, 1982, pp. 30–31)

We are interested in the role that PAR methodologies can play in the development of educational materials for art teachers to teach toward a heightened awareness of how civic engagement plays out in the lives of young people. The nested design of this study allows the teens to act as participants in the broader framework, as they explore and contribute both directly and indirectly to the development of a civically engaged art curriculum (Cammarota & Fine, 2010). By positioning the students as researchers (SAR), we called upon the SAR approach put forward by Fielding (2001). Fielding proposes that SAR is "a transformative, 'transversal' approach in which the voices of students, teachers and significant others involved in the process of education construct ways of working that are emancipatory in both process and outcome" (2001, p. 124). SAR projects support civic engagement, as they forward both research and educational practice while supporting student agency. This model of participatory research design is increasingly common when studying issues related to social justice in education (Smyth & McInerney, 2012; Smyth et al., 2014). By positioning the teen participants as researchers, we hoped to engender a sense of ownership in the process as they inquired into and engaged the history of the civil rights movement in Tallahassee.

Background

In our five years of researching and working together, we have discovered that by giving students access and tools, they are able to do the complex work of situating themselves in a community, and connecting community histories to present conditions (Fendler & Shields, 2018). This experience gave us insight into how artmaking, combined with locally based inquiry, encourages young people to engage their world in new ways. As a result, we were eager to explore ways to formalize this process and purposefully design a curriculum built around meaningful locally based, artistic inquiries, intentionally guiding students toward understanding how they might become more civically engaged. The resulting curricular project brought together local teens during the summers of 2018 and 2019 (Fendler et al., 2020; Shields et al., 2020). Each summer we offered a week-long intensive art program to upper-middle and high school students focused on studying and reflecting on the legacy of the civil rights movement in Tallahassee, Florida. The 2018 and 2019 summer programs ran for a period of 5 full days in mid-July from 7:30 am to 5:00 pm and were free for participating students. To gather prospective students, we invited art teachers from all public and charter middle and high schools in the area to nominate two students. We received approximately 25 nominations each year, and while all nominated students were invited, not all participated. In 2018, 12 students completed the program, and, in 2019, 16 students completed it, 4 of whom were returning students from the previous year. Of these students, around 60% were students of color and 40% were White students.

This summer program, *Tallahassee Foot Soldiers. Change Makers: Then and Now*, focused on teaching the legacy of the civil rights movement through local people, places, and events. In developing this project, we expanded on the critical moments of our earlier, less formal, collaboration with teens and were guided by the fields of art education, history, and civics. We used all of this to inform the creation of opportunities for students to move through the city, talk to community members, connect with materials, and grapple with their experiences through artmaking. Our summer program developed a curriculum whose primary content was the city itself, allowing students to learn about a place *in* that place. We wanted to use the immediacy of our local community to engage students in an experience of living history. We focused on the ways in which history could be brought to life for students, by making it contemporary, tangible, and connected to the present. This history is less apparent in the local school curriculum, as classroom resources tend to take a broader, national view of the civil rights movement. While we are sensitive to the fact that teachers may not be experts on their community's history, we believe students can be invited to do history without requiring teachers to occupy the role of experts. Meaning, the teacher/researchers in our program learned alongside the students, a decision reflected in our theoretical and methodological beliefs about research practices. We went into this project believing that the invitation to learn about community history through local research should be central. This engages students in the project of producing knowledge through research, where they think like historians, make like contemporary artists, and act like community members. With this loose template of thinking, making, and acting, we packed our bookbags, filled our water bottles, and headed out to explore Tallahassee.

Tallahassee and the legacy of the civil rights movement

Tallahassee, the state capital of Florida, has a population of approximately 193,000 people, 56.5% of whom are White, 35% of whom are Black, 4.5% of whom are Asian, and 4% of whom identify as multi- or bi-racial, Native American, Native Hawaiian or Pacific Islander, or Other. The city is home to Florida State University (FSU) and Florida Agricultural and Mechanical University (FAMU), which is the second largest Historically Black College & University (HBCU) in the nation. As a historic site,

Tallahassee was the only Southern capital city east of the Mississippi that was not captured during the Civil War, allowing it to resume robust economic activity during the era of Reconstruction. During this time, the Black population of the city rose significantly and several Black neighborhoods were established and flourished. This economic growth supported the development of middle-class communities of color, where Black people owned homes and businesses. Residents from these communities, in conjunction with students and faculty at FAMU, went on to lead and sustain local actions in support of the civil rights movement.

Several key moments characterized the civil rights movement in the city. Only a few months after Rosa Parks inspired the first bus boycott in Montgomery, Alabama, Tallahassee initiated its own. In May 1956, two FAMU students, Wilhelmina Jakes and Carrie Patterson, declined to give up their seats to White passengers. They were arrested and the next morning, Reverend C.K. Steele, representative of the National Association for the Advancement of Colored People (NAACP), visited the two women at their shared home and extended the NAACP's support. That same night, after the local newspaper printed their address, members of the Ku Klux Klan burned a cross in their yard. Jakes and Patterson sought safety on the FAMU campus for the night, where the news of the cross-burning spread quickly. The Student Government Association at FAMU voted to begin a bus boycott in response, and the community rallied in support (Uhl & Evans, 2021). Rev. C.K. Steele emerged as a local leader, and with community members, developed the Inter-Civic Council (ICC). The ICC represented the interest of the boycotters at the municipal level and beyond. Rev. C. K. Steele went on to become a national figure in the civil rights movement, and was elected as the first Vice President of the Southern Christian Leadership Conference (SCLC). The SCLC was a Christian-based supporter of the civil rights movement and was part of what was nationally known as the "Big Five:" the National Association for the Advancement of Colored People (NAACP), the National Urban League (NUL), the Student Nonviolent Coordinating Committee (SNCC), and the Congress on Racial Equality (CORE).

After months of resistance from the city, all of the ICC's demands were ultimately met. The central participation of FAMU students, who both instigated the boycott and assisted in volunteer and organizing efforts that sustained it, provided a model for the ways in which student efforts could become central to the movement. Historians have credited the central role of the FAMU student body as inspiring the development of The Student Nonviolent Coordinating Committee (SNCC) (Padgett & Dawkins, 1998). The boycott was successful and had an impact in the national movement, marking Tallahassee as a significant "movement center" akin to the impact of events in Montgomery (Padgett & Dawkins, 1998,

p. 101). After the success of the boycott, the community continued to leverage the structures of support it had developed, continuing its formidable role in a national movement. Two FAMU students and sisters, Patricia Stephens Due and Priscilla Stephens Kruize, are credited with opening a chapter of CORE in Tallahassee, where the ICC, under leadership of Rev. C. K. Steele, provided administrative and financial support. In February 1960, CORE protesters were arrested after a lunch counter sit-in, and enacted the movement's first jail-in, which garnered national media attention. This protest tactic was widely adopted by SNCC. A year later, in 1961, members of the Interfaith Freedom Riders stopped in Tallahassee, and were subsequently arrested when entering a segregated restaurant at the Tallahassee airport on the day of their departure. Once again Tallahassee was in the national news, reporting on the arrests of the Tallahassee 10 (State Archives of Florida, n.d.). In 1963, large demonstrations against segregation organized by FAMU students led to mass arrests of dozens of people in May and, later, of 350 people in September, prompting the city to hold protesters in a makeshift prison at the state fairgrounds.

In the political arena, LeRoy Collins, governor of Florida from 1955 to 1961, was another important figure. Although he campaigned as a segregationist, once in office he took a strong public stance in favor of desegregation. After the *Brown v. Board of Education* ruling in 1957, Collins criticized the Florida legislature for their resistance toward school desegregation, using a pragmatic legal argument. In 1960, he made a public speech claiming segregation was morally wrong. After leaving office, Collins became a prominent national figure, and was appointed by President Johnson to serve as Director of the Community Relations Service (CRS), a federal agency established by Title X of the Civil Rights Act. As a prominent Southern White politician and businessman, the role Collins played in modeling a movement toward desegregation was impactful throughout the state. As a Tallahassee native, his presence is felt in the city that honors his name and legacy.

The history of Tallahassee is rich with events, activists, organizations, politicians, and legislation that are a reflection of key moments in the national civil rights movement. Importantly, this history is still alive in the city, where past activists are current residents, monuments and historical markers reference key events, and the state archives catalog many of these historical moments through primary source document collections. In this way, the city serves as a resource for curriculum, for artmaking, for learning, and ultimately for becoming a community member. If we engage with it, it can teach students, in captivating and tangible ways, about the people, places, and events that contributed to the story of social justice in Tallahassee and beyond. In this way, "all people and peoples are living histories" and we come from other moments, stories, experiences, events, and places, "so understanding the linkages between past and present is absolutely basic for a good understanding of the condition of being human" (Corfield, 2007, pp. 1–2).

A curriculum built on inquiry into living history

Our curriculum centered on people, places, and events in an effort to explore a complex era. We worked to design engaging entry points that combined primary sources and first-person perspectives. Because of the person-centeredness of the civil rights movement, we began with people. Our own introduction to the civil rights movement was the Tallahassee Heritage Walk, a monument that commemorates the foot soldiers, or civil rights activists, from Tallahassee. The monument consists of a series of terrazzo sidewalk panels, which names over 50 people who participated in the city's bus boycott and the actions and protests that took place in the 1960s (see Figure 4.1). For each person named there, we created a curriculum resource, or case file. The case files served as prompts for inquiry, with each one giving students a person's name, a key characteristic, a list of important facts, two leading questions, and a small selection of archival images. The program began by asking students to select a case file, introducing them to the history of the civil rights movement through a person-first perspective. The case files gave students an anchor through which to begin their exploration of historic events making up the civil rights movement (see Figure 4.1).

In addition to focusing on names from the past, our program relied on the physical presence of community members. Each summer we invited local activists to talk to our students about their participation in the civil rights movement, bringing to life their decisions to take part in this social movement. Whether the conversations were in our campus classroom or a neighborhood backyard, the dialogue that unfolded in these sessions was impactful. We heard students asking the activists about their experiences, their decisions, and what options are available to them today. Their presence in the classroom and the stories they told our students helped thread the needle between the past and present, inviting students to feel connected to history. We selected activists that highlighted the central role of young people in the civil rights movement, first inviting Henry Steele, who was put in jail as a high school student for his participation in the sit-ins. We also hosted a group of women, led by Gloria Anderson, who organized and executed the first Woolworth lunch counter sit-in in Tallahassee, an event that was never formally documented by the media and, thus, almost forgotten in historical accounts. We were invited to sit in the backyard of Annie Harris, who was a local artist and a teacher in an area high school during desegregation, and her friend, Daryl Scott, whose father helped organize Martin Luther King Jr.'s nonviolent training in Tallahassee. We also invited

Figure 4.1 Collage of students engaging in the weekly activities

local artists, members of neighborhood associations, and educators from museums and the state archives to expand the conversation and engage students through dialogue.

While people, both past and present, brought the stories of the civil rights movement to life, we grounded our explorations in the places where their stories unfolded. In this way, places served as a second touchstone of our work with the teens. Again, expanding out from the Tallahassee Heritage Walk monument, we identified significant places in town that held memories of historical moments: a church that Rev. CK Steele preached at, a bus station dedicated to the bus boycotts, a street sign with the names of Wilhelmina Jakes and Carrie Patterson, one of the oldest historically Black neighborhoods in Florida, a historical marker on FAMU's campus, and so on. Other places were chosen for the collections and objects they held. The State Archives made available a large, curated collection of documents pertaining to the civil rights movement (see Figure 4.1). The Meek-Eaton Black Archives and Museum allowed students to come face-to-face with art and artifacts that told complex stories about the Black experience, through a narrative situating the civil rights movement inside a wider timeline. For the first few days of the week, our curriculum and classroom became the city. As we explored the city, we noted which historic places were missing, notably, the Woolworth building, where the sit-ins took place, and the county jail where activists were held. Prior to bringing teens to these sites, we mapped how we would access this wide range of places, relying on local bus lines and places that we could walk to from our classroom on FSU's campus (see Figure 4.1). As much as possible, we relied on walking to give our students insight into how historic places fit into the present geography and how the movement moved along city streets. The walking added another layer of context and provided a necessary entry point to accessing historical moments that existed before Tallahassee became a commuter city. The indelible heat and humidity were also protagonists in this experience, as we asked students to be out in the world in a way that challenged how these people from history might have typically experienced the city in the peak of summer.

The places we visited introduced the events that took place in them, providing a final layer to contextualize the civil rights movement as an event belonging to our local history. In this way, events provided a framework for this project, in terms of both our content and the teens conceptual understanding. Looking closely at people and places, we introduced small moments that gave insight into the objectives, challenges, and successes of the larger movement. Through this lens, we approached history as a series of interconnected local events where individual actions lead into another, and eventually built into a movement. Daily, we asked students to reflect on what they learned about the civil rights movement and how it was relevant to them, and to today. As we pushed back against a vision of history as something detached from the present, we witnessed the teens feel the significance of history in their own lives, making connections between the movement and contemporary struggles for racial justice, LGBTQ equality, or family history.

As we explore in more detail in the forthcoming chapters in Section 3 of our volume, the living presence of history—history students could talk to, stand in, and touch—invited students to place themselves within an unfolding narrative of the present. Students learned about the past in ways that felt personal and meaningful for their future. Furthermore, they were asked to compile and reflect this information through inquiry-based processes, deepening their learning experience and promoting civic agency.

Think | make | act: Curriculum strategies that blend art and civics

At the start of this chapter we shared how we observed the impact that place-based, artistic projects had on the civic engagement opportunities of young people. Through this observation, we saw an opportunity to advocate for the powerful role art education can have in supporting civic education. As discussed in Chapter 1, civic education relies on a three-part model that teaches knowledge, values, and skills. The education of engaged citizens is built around asking young people to obtain knowledge of civic processes, gain experience taking part in these processes, and develop a value system that invites them to understand the relationship between self-interest and the greater good. While the qualities of civic education are well known, it remains difficult to implement in schools, where curriculum tends to overemphasize teaching content, while spending less time on skills and dispositions. We believe that art, as a subject based on practice, is an area where the continued development of skills and dispositions can take place. In Chapter 3, we suggested that students be asked to think, make, and act, allowing artmaking to become the fulcrum of a learning process that moves students from a mode of inquiry and reflection, an active mode of expression and intervention. As explored in Chapter 3 of this volume, artmaking is a complex process that collapses distinctions between thinking, making, and acting. Students think and learn while manipulating materials, students express themselves while making, which is a form of action, and so on. Integrating contemporary arts-based inquiry into the classroom is a context through which students can engage in many of the civic competencies we seek to teach our students. The following sections serve to tease apart this approach, offering a detailed look at what curricular materials we developed in support of a think | make | act model.

Thinking: Scaffolding student research with field guides

Our summer program relied on a curriculum field guide, or workbook filled with self-guided exercises and reflection prompts related to our day-to-day activities. The field guide supported self-directed learning by allowing students to move through the activities at their own pace. It also functioned as a place for students to collect their notes, emerging ideas, and sketches, while responding to the day's activities. In the social sciences, the field guide is a foundational tool for researchers to process the events of fieldwork, making connections, and moving thinking forward. They served the same function in our curricular context. The curriculum field guide was not a blank slate for students. It followed the linear progression of the curriculum and included background information, activities, and reflection prompts.

For site visits, it offered historical context and suggested ways of observing and registering places through artmaking, prompting activities such as making rubbings or taking photographs. Pages dedicated to the state archives and the Meek-Eaton Black Archive and Museum offered background information, procedures, and protocols for visiting the collection, and suggested activities for finding materials, taking notes, and sketching. Other pages provided information about guest speakers and prompted students to develop questions to ask them. The most prominent feature of the field guides was a series of reflection prompts, which appeared daily, asking students what stood out to them, what connections they were drawing between the past and present, and how their individual projects were taking shape. The field guide culminated with a space to draft an artist statement to compliment the final piece.

By working through the prompts in the field guides, students did not simply consume the information our program provided but deepened their understanding as they documented how the information changed their thinking and making. While students did not complete every activity listed in the field guides, they provided each student space for compiling and completing research, as well as space for reflecting. Ultimately, the field guide prompted students to engage in deep thinking, capturing how they were responding to and processing the information they were encountering during the program. Our aim with the field guide was to provide a template for students to begin the work of doing—historical and artistic research—rather than just receiving information about art and history. In this way, field guides were a space for synthesis and analysis. As students engaged with primary sources, site visits, or invited talks, their field guide accompanied them. Reading through them, we found they did not offer information but asked students to produce it, by providing choice, flexibility, and space to document thinking.

Making: Creatively remixing the past in the present

Just as we borrowed the field guide from qualitative research, we borrowed another framing phrase from a contemporary creative lexicon, the remix. The concept of remixing was familiar to young people and helped scaffold arts-based research into studio practice. Our program worked to approach history by framing the significance of the past in the present. To prompt students to make these connections, we drew on the artistic practice of creative remixing. Midway through the week, we showed students examples from film, music videos, songs, and contemporary art to consider how artists sample existing material in order to layer meaning into their work. We looked at how artists use primary source materials, symbols, and visual references, and how a new context can alter the meaning of original material. After viewing the contemporary examples, we asked students to document what they were remixing in their own work. This question was prompted in the field guides and through discussion, where we asked students to articulate what they were remixing during our in-process critiques.

At each location we visited, we also asked students to engage in some sort of material exploration. At the bus stop, we gave them photographs from the bus boycotts and asked them to try and locate the site of the memory. Using a photography technique called rephotography, students held the archival image up and photographed the two moments in time together (for a discussion of rephotography see Chapter 5). At Bethel Baptist Church and the Tallahassee Heritage Walk, we asked the teens to do rubbings using crayons and newsprint. When we were invited into the backyard of a longtime Tallahassee resident to sit and listen to her recall her experience during the desegregation of Tallahassee schools, the teens used their phone cameras to photograph and record the conversation as it evolved. The field guides housed all of these activities, prompting the teens at each juncture in our week.

During the last two days we dedicated the full time allotted to making art. We asked the teens to reflect on what they saw and encountered by prompting them to bridge their research with their artmaking, identifying the moments that glowed from earlier in the week. The concept of glowing data was a term we borrowed from the social sciences, where MacClure (2010, 2020) wrote about approaching data analysis by honing in on data that glow. For MacClure, the data that glow are not processed through systematic comparisons of a large data set, instead, they refer to the way in which some data can reach out and capture the researcher in meaningful ways. To follow data that glow is to allow an inquiry process to be guided by affective responses, heeding points of interest that take us in unexpected directions. When we invited students into this arts-based research process, we did not expect them to engage all the information they encountered; rather, we hoped that they would respond to a glow in something they came across during the programmed activities.

These dual acts of remixing and identifying data that glowed gave students a framework for turning their artmaking into a research process.

Students were asked to anchor their artwork in the primary source material, where the notion of remix pushed students beyond producing representational work, by asking them to respond to the history they were learning and doing. We guided the teens actively during the two days of full-time artmaking, asking them to step back and forth, consider what the work was saying, and avoiding artistic choices that simply illustrated history through representational visuals. This became the role of the teacher/ researcher, to identify when students needed guidance by constantly asking questions and prompting reflection. The teacher/researchers, also served as subject experts, giving students the skills, tools, and knowledge that were necessary to make a linoleum print, create a mixed-media painting, or sew a doll. We saw our job as facilitators of experiences, offering suggestions for mediums, pulling up contemporary artists their work reminded us of, or prompting students to step back and think about their next steps.

   We also integrated the critique process into every step of the making process. We asked students to engage in several group critique sessions daily, pushing them to look at each other's work and offer feedback, guidance, and suggestions. At the end of each of the critique sessions, students closed by sharing what feedback they were considering incorporating, what their next steps might be, and what their goal for the day was. These formative moments offered opportunities for the teens to stay focused by creating goals and plans for following through with ideas. By prompting these moments of critical reflection and artistic decision making, the work the teens produced moved beyond illustrations of the past and began to juxtapose the past with the present, all while situating their own stories in relation to a growing understanding of historical context. Through this process, the work of making became a project of knowledge creation and moved students to see themselves, their families, stories, and experiences in relation to the history of their community; an artistic action that began to develop a sense of belonging and connection to the Tallahassee community.

Acting: Setting the stage for transformation

Chapter 3 showed that research points to the need for classroom activities to extend beyond the school setting, positioning students as actors in their community in meaningful ways. However, given the constraints placed on schools, this step can often seem like a stretch. In our own program, we felt this constraint mostly in relation to time: our interaction with students was limited to just one week. While several students returned for a second summer, the condensed time we spent with students did not allow us to observe how this program impacted their long-term civic engagement. We can, however, use their artwork, reflections, and closing interviews to speculate how the experience impacted their civic agency.

As educators, we often observe the fluctuating nature of students' capacities and constraints. Therefore, we understand agency as both temporal and relational; we believe the ability to make decisions and impact the community is not an immutable quality but is a possibility that depends on both external and internal factors. Biesta and Tedder (2007) acknowledged that self-reflection on the "particular ecology" (p. 137) of agency can aid individuals in understanding their own situations and, possibly, help guide them toward more future-leaning orientations. One that emphasizes purpose over present concerns or past routines, in order to change "our responsiveness to the situations we encounter in our lives" (p. 146). It is in this space of reflection and responsiveness that we saw our project operating. In the summer program, students studied history in order to understand the present. They were positioned as knowledge producers as they pieced together a vision of the historical struggle for civil rights, they were encouraged to talk about their own struggles and learn from others that confronted and addressed social injustices. This was an ecology that allowed students to achieve agency in their learning process and supported an orientation toward the future as rooted in past success. This push for action or change, as the quintessential component of civic agency, is often viewed as the ability to enact meaningful change in the community; however, the possibility of change cannot exist without a sense of ownership or commitment to the community. We believe that in the face of our big ask—tasking students to become civic actors later—our program led students to develop a perspective on themselves, their community, and the history of social movements, which could inspire them to take purposeful actions and decisions. This is not to say that you cannot scaffold toward community projects in a classroom, but rather that the process of becoming a community member should be viewed as an essential element in the larger project of teaching toward civic engagement.

In Chapter 3, we briefly discussed the ways that community learning and service learning projects put young people in the community as civic tourists, not committed and engaged members of that community. We see the potential for projects like this one to ask students to do the work of learning about their community's history and use artmaking to paint, draw, sculpt, and weave themselves into history. We believe the action of becoming a community member lays the foundation for future investment and engagement, transforming young people into participants in the world. The deeply complex and time-consuming work of changing communities must start small, with the seeds of change just beginning to germinate. This project does the work of tending the soil, digging the hole, and planting the seed; trusting that when the project ends, growing still unfolds. That these young people will look at their city differently, they will recognize street names and the people they commemorate, be able to identify historical sites, share these important events with their friends and family, and perhaps some of them will stay in Tallahassee and become the future police chief, mayor, school board member, or gallery director. Our hope is that through the work of thinking and making like a historian, artist, and community member, they nurtured their own sense of belonging, formed their own attachments to places, and will continue to find ways to learn about and invest in the future of their communities. Just as we framed history as a process of events, large and small, we approached learning the same way. While asking students to take action in their learning—to *do* history, to be arts based researchers—we asked them to engage in events, to be community members.

Conclusion

With neither researcher from Tallahassee, it is important to note that our curriculum also mirrored our own process of discovery as we began to study Tallahassee's history and make connections to the present. This project was an opportunity for both the teacher/researchers and the teens to learn more about their community and begin to see themselves as part of it. In this project we sought to formulate a civically engaged art curriculum that was contextually bound and artistically imagined; and as curriculum designers, we underlie the importance of placing the student's lived experience and relationships with their communities at the center of the learning experience. All of this with the ultimate goal of working with students to create opportunities to come into an individualized and local understanding of civic participation and engagement. "The immediate focus of such pedagogy is taken to emerge dialogically between the particular interests of local students and the objectives of the educator, and it centers on consideration of the texts, artifacts, and performances of local cultural production" (Ball & Lai, 2006, p. 262).

This critical pedagogy of place holds the relationships among social, cultural, ecological, and political issues at the center of curriculum development efforts. This critical view of students and their civic engagement environment helps emphasize and highlight the issues of inequity and access that are currently lacking in many curricular models (Graham, 2007). Similarly, when considering an art curriculum, we see a demonstrated need for art classrooms to become sites where the student and teacher become artists that think collaboratively about their communities, and that use the conceptual materials of people, places, and events to think and do history, make art, and act as community members. In this way, the impact of a civically engaged art curricula might lie in its ability to empower students to investigate local communities and view those spaces as the settings for their own civic participation. This assumption brings us to the end of our discussion of the details of the curricular model by providing a brief overview of the daily encounters for students. In the next chapter, we share a day-by-day discussion of the experiences the teen participants, in hopes of painting a fuller picture of this project.

References

Ball, E. L., & Lai, A. (2006). Place-based pedagogy for the arts and humanities. *Pedagogy*, 6(2), 261–287. Duke University Press. https://doi.org/10.1215/15314200-2005-004

Biesta, G., & Tedder, M. (2007). Agency and learning in the life course: Towards an ecological perspective. *Studies in the Education of Adults*, 39(2), 132–149. https://doi.org/10.1080/02660830.2007.11661545

Cammarota, J., & Fine, M. (2010). Youth participatory action research: A pedagogy for transformational resistance. In *Revolutionizing education* (pp. 9–20). Routledge. https://doi.org/10.4324/9780203932100

Corfield, P. J. (2007). *All people are living histories—Which is why history matters.* London University's Institute of Historical Research. https://www.penelopejcorfield.com/PDFs/6.1.1-CorfieldPdf1-Why-History-Matters.pdf

Fendler, R., & Shields, S. S. (2018). Filming Frenchtown: Listening to and learning from storied lives. *Learning Landscapes*, 11(2), 141–155. https://doi.org/10.36510/learnland.v11i2.952

Fendler, R., Shields, S. S., & Henn, D. (2020). #thefutureisnow: A model for civically engaged art education. *Art Education*, 73(5), 10–15. https://doi.org/10.1080/00043125.2020.1766922

Fielding, M. (2001). Students as radical agents of change. *Journal of Educational Change*, 2(2), 123–141. https://doi.org/10.1023/a:1017949213447

Friere, P. (1982). Creating alternative research methods. Learning to do it by doing it. In B. Hall, A. Gillette, & R. Tandon (Eds.), *Creating knowledge: A monopoly* (pp. 29–37). Society for Participatory Research in Asia.

Friere, P. (1970). *Pedagogy of the oppressed.* Continuum.

Graham, M. A. (2007). Art, ecology and art education: Locating art education in a critical place-based pedagogy. *Studies in Art Education*, 48(4), 375–391. https://doi.org/10.1080/00393541.2007.11650115

MacClure, M. (2010). The offence of theory. *Journal of Education Policy*, 25(2), 275–283. https://doi.org/10.1080/02680930903462316

MacClure, M. (2020). Inquiry as divination. *Qualitative Inquiry*, 23(4), 345–370. https://doi.org/10.1177/1077800420939124

Orfield, G., & Ee, J. (2017). Patterns of resegregation in Florida's school [A Report for the LeRoy Collins Institute, Florida State University]. Los Angeles, CA: The Civil Rights Project-Proyecto Derechos Civiles at UCLA.

Padgett, G., & Dawkins, M. (1998). Tallahassee's bus protest: The other boycott that sparked the civil rights movement. *The Negro Educational Review*, 49(3), 101–106.

Peng, C. Y. J. (2004). Nested design. In M. S. Lewis-Beck, A. E. Bryman, & T. F. Liao (Eds.), *The SAGE encyclopedia of social science research methods* (pp. 717–719). Sage Publications. https://doi.org/10.4135/9781412950589

Shields, S. S., Fendler, R., & Henn, D. (2020). A vision of civically engaged art education: Teens as arts-based researchers. *Studies in Art Education*, 61(2), 123–141. https://doi.org/10.1080/00393541.2020.1740146

Smyth, J., & McInerney, P. (2012). *Silent witnesses to active agents: Student voice in re-engaging with learning.* Peter Lang.

Smyth, J., Down, B., & McInerney, P. (2014). The socially just school: Making space for youth to speak back. Springer. https://doi.org/10.1007/978-94-017-9060-4

State Archives of Florida. (n.d.). Primary source set: The Tallahassee Ten. Florida Memory Project. https://www.floridamemory.com/items/show/340611

Uhl, S., & Evans, H. (2021). *Black history month: The story of the Tallahassee Bus Boycott.* Florida State University, Department of History. https://history.fsu.edu/article/black-history-month-story-tallahassee-bus-boycott

5   Curriculum Overview

Introduction

This section is abbreviated, but we think it is necessary for understanding the case studies in the upcoming chapters in Section III. While Chapter 4 gave a macro-overview of the curricular design this project took, this chapter does the work of detailing the daily activities of the students and teacher/researchers. We spend time here offering the details of the activities and trips in hopes of inspiring others to explore their own communities. Neither of us are from Tallahassee, so we spent time walking through the city before we began the project. We visited the state archives and Meek-Eaton Black Archives, where we found educators that enthusiastically invited us to visit with the students. We visited neighborhoods, attended art openings, and networked with local schools to identify people, places, and events critical to the project. We scoured local newspapers for events that featured the history of civil rights in Tallahassee, learning about road dedications, the development of historic markers, and public speaking events. We visited the public library and looked at books, focused on civil rights in Florida, written by Florida residents. The more we looked, the more volumes and articles we found written by people with roots that still exist in Tallahassee. We toured the history museum and visited parks. We rode the bus to many of these locations in an attempt to learn the bus routes. We did exactly what we asked the teens to do, we got to know Tallahassee. In this process, we developed a connection with our city that is hard to explain. As transplants, we both came here to work for Florida State University, and after this project, we see ourselves as committed, invested civic participants. This is perhaps a testament to the potential this type of project holds. When you really get to know the place you live in, it becomes yours. The streets are familiar, the sounds soothing, and the unfolding list of community events becomes ways to deepen your relationship. We hope you consider doing this work as well, start by taking

DOI: 10.4324/9781003199106-7

a walk or visiting a place you have never been, talk to a stranger in line at the grocery store, or turn the radio up when you hear talk about local events. As you tune in to the place you live in, we challenge you to grab this chapter, pack some art materials, and use some of the activities as inspiration for ways to creatively engage in getting to know your own city, town, or neighborhoods.

Day one

On the first day of the summer sessions, students met in a large auditorium. They completed the ice-breaker activity that asked them to get into small groups and identify three or four things they have in common. They also completed the pre-assessment questions, asking them to share what they already knew about the civil rights movement generally and specifically here in Tallahassee. Then, as a group, they watched the latest updates on the recently reopened Emmett Till trial and reflected in their field guides about how they were feeling. Afterward, we jumped right in, walking to the bus station and Bethel Baptist Church, where students participated in a rephotography activity. Rephotography is "revisiting a historic image to take a new photograph from the same point of view... [it] opens up new avenues for research. It also helps redefine our relationship to the past and the future" (Faber, 2019, n.p.). Photographers like Seth Taras, Jim Adams, and Ricard Martínez use this approach to juxtapose historic photographs with contemporary locations. This process gives the viewer a glimpse at what historic locations look like in the present day. Similarly, our activity asked students to take a historic image from the civil rights movement in Tallahassee and try to find the location of the event in the bus station or near Bethel Baptist Church. Then using their phones, they were asked to hold the image in front of them and take a picture that juxtaposes the historic image with the modern-day location (see Figure 5.1 for the field guide page). We ended the morning at the Tallahassee Heritage Walk in downtown Tallahassee, where students were given crayons and paper to take rubbings and choose their case files (see Figure 5.2 for the field guide page). Since the case files represented the individuals featured on the heritage walk, we thought making connections between the case files and their names commemorated on the sidewalk would be an exciting first connection. We then traveled to the state archives, where the students had three hours to explore the archives in search of connections to their case files (see Figure 5.3 for the field guide page). Upon returning to campus, we spent an hour decompressing, making a small collage with the artifacts from the day, and completing reflections in the field guides.

Figure 5.1 Rephotography guide from the student field guides

Day two

Day two began with a pre-assessment activity that asked students to share what they know about civil protest and the concept of nonviolent activism. Specifically, students were asked to share what they know about sit-ins and protest posters. Like the collage activity from the day before, this

Figure 5.2 Field guide page with checklist for student engagement at sites

day also included some low-stakes artmaking activities. We began in the studio classroom and worked with mono-printing on Gelli plates to create stickers focused on activism, featuring a takeaway or glowing concept from the day before. To make these stickers, students were introduced to the work of Favianna Rodriguez, as they discussed how art can be used to convey a message. (For a detailed description and an expansion on the relevance of Rodriguez's work, see Chapter 10.) Students worked in small groups to generate nouns that describe a glowing concept from the day before and then brainstorm verbs that represent actions that could be taken to change or address the problems and concepts from the day before. The small groups came together and posted these into a larger class list that became a resource for students to use. The teens then worked individually to select nouns and verbs from the large list to begin to come up with a simple and direct statement or slogan that represented their takeaway or glowing data from the previous day. The teens did a guided activity helping them understand how symbols could be used to convey a message and

Hunting in the Archives....

How to do Archival Research:
- SKIM
- Look for:
  - ❏ Keywords
  - ❏ Location (is there a place associated with the article? Is it relevant to your File?)
  - ❏ Who wrote it? (Someone your person knows?)
  - ❏ Who's it for? (Someone your person knows?)
  - ❏ Who is mentioned in the document?
  - ❏ What institutions are listed in the document?
- If your document checks a box, then happy hunting!
- Don't have time to read it all? Take a Picture!
  - Write the Series, Box, and Folder numbers on a slip of paper.
  - Include it in the picture so when you're browsing through your phone later, you know where it came from!

Think about this:
Pay attention to the way they talk about African-Americans and Civil Rights issues. Is it the same that we talk about it today?

Things to look for:
- Facts
- Examples
- Statistics
- Cool photographs
- Author quotes
- Little known ideas/events/thoughts
- Expert opinions and counter opinions
- Stuff you find interesting

12

Figure 5.3 Field guide page with notes for how to work in the state archives

were challenged to develop symbols that represented their statements and slogans. Students used the remaining time to create a small set of mono-printed stickers with the symbols and slogans to be used the next day (for samples of student work, see Figure 5.4).

During our break, students were briefed on our visiting guest; in 2018, this was Henry Steele and in 2019 it was Gloria Anderson and Bernice

Figure 5.4 Three examples of student's monoprint stickers

Presley, both sit-in participants. Henry Steele, Gloria Anderson, and Bernice Presley were teen participants in local marches, sit-ins, demonstrations, mass meetings, and court hearings during the Civil Rights Movement in Tallahassee. Prior to their arrival, students were asked to generate three questions to ask and then given space to take notes from the conversation. When our guests arrived, each of the students introduced themselves and gave a brief overview of the case file they had selected and a recap of what they had learned so far. Then we opened the floor to an informal conversation about activism during the civil rights movement, with specific attention to what it was like to be a teen participating in the movement. Each of the guests offered an overview of their early lives and how they became involved in the movement, sharing memories of their experiences with the teens. These conversations opened up, allowing students to ask questions and continue the dialogue. Once the guest visits concluded, we spent the afternoon in the computer lab using Canva.com to design posters that were loosely based on the lessons and key takeaways from the previous day and the guest speakers. We closed the day by printing the posters and asking students to reflect on what they learned and how they might apply that learning.

Day three

Like our previous days, day three began with a pre-assessment activity where students were asked to think of artists or musicians who used the past as inspiration. The third day marks our transition into the arts, as we begin to explore how artists use history to inform their work. After a few minutes of working in their field guides, the students divided into groups and left to walk around campus and find locations to post their posters and stickers from the previous day. Students were asked to think about where they were putting their posters and how the location impacts the ways the message might be received. After traversing campus in small groups, all the groups met up at the bus stop near campus and rode to the Meek-Eaton Black Archives on Florida A&M's campus. The Meek-Eaton Black Archives serve as a research center and museum collecting, displaying, and preserving artifacts from Black history and culture in the Southeastern United States. Their unique collection of historical documents, artifacts, and artwork is used to support research and public education. The students were taken on a guided tour of the museum, laying the groundwork for expanding their understanding of the civil rights movement in Tallahassee to include a local, national, and global perspective. This provided the necessary context for understanding the movement. Later that day, students spent the afternoon talking with local activist artists. In 2018, we visited Annie Harris, an activist and artist in the historically Black Frenchtown community, and in 2019, artists Sarah Painter, Cosby Hayes, and Adreenah Wynn visited campus to talk about their activism and/or mural work across the state of Florida. During their visits, students once again generated and shared questions, asking the artists about how art provides opportunities to participate in communities and share ideas, messages, and information with the public. After their visits students were introduced to the artistic concept of remix through artists like Nick Cave, Kevin Beasley, and Willie Cole. (For a detailed description and exploration of some of their work see Chapter 10.) Students were asked to think about what personal stories, concepts, ideas, histories, memories, observations, and reflections they might remix as they revisited their glowing data from earlier in the week (see Figure 5.5).

Like our other days, this day concluded with artmaking and some additional time for students to begin talking in small groups about the artwork they wanted to make during the last two days of the week. These conversations centered around a series of questions about remixing, a discussion of project designs, and then small group consideration and feedback. The general flow of this critique session was as follows:

1 What kind of remix is interesting to you? (song, image, artifact …)
2 What medium is interesting to you? (video, sound, song, paint, print-making, etc.)
3 How would you define remix in the context of your ideas?
4 Sketch out (using words and/or images) what your ideas are for your final project. Consider these questions:

   a What will it look/sound/feel like?
   b What materials will help it look/sound/feel the way you want it to?
   c What is special about this material and how will you use it to help you communicate?

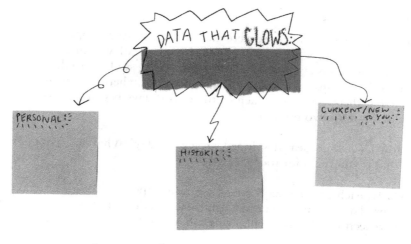

Figure 5.5 Excerpt from field guide prompting students to identify glowing data

5 In your small groups do the following:

   a Share your project design ideas and brainstorming
   b Share and get feedback, consider the following questions as you give your peers feedback:

      i What is working?
      ii What is too much or too obvious?
      iii Where can they scale back?
      iv What can they add?
      v What can they take away?
      vi Where can they zoom in?
      vii Where can they zoom out?
      viii How might this be interpreted?
      ix How might this be misinterpreted?
      x How can this become compelling without becoming cliche?

6 After the small group feedback, rework and get a plan for tomorrow. Pay attention to the following:

   a What do you need from us? (printers, paint, specific materials, etc.)
   b What will you do to get started in the morning?
   c How are you using the concept of creative remix in your project?
   d What is your plan for tomorrow?

Days four and five

The last two days of the week were identical in format and open in nature. These last two days gave students two full days of working time. The teacher/researchers circulated the room prompting students to think about their work and push their ideas. The students sat where they wanted and worked at their own pace. Each of these workdays began with students' consideration of two prompts:

1 How have your ideas developed since yesterday? What has changed?
2 What is your plan for today?

Similarly, each of these days contained four opportunities for critical reflections. Two of these were independent reflections and two were small group reflections. All four reflections contained the same prompting:

1 What is working well?
2 What are you having trouble with?
3 What help do you need from others?

At the end of each of the group reflections, students shared their work and their responses to the same feedback questions from day three. These moments for both independent and guided reflection reinforced the artistic practice of pause and distance, by asking students to stop, step away and consider the next steps. When they arrived on the last morning, day five, they took some time to share their feelings about their artwork and list three concrete goals for completing their work that day. During the last day, we also asked students to join us in groups of two or three to answer the final interview and reflection questions.

1 Why do you think it is important that historical moments are recorded?
2 Can you tell me about what role you played in the week-long workshop?
3 Can you list and discuss some of the major themes you focused on in your part of the project?
4 What was something you learned about Tallahassee?
5 What was something that surprised you?
6 Think about a specific experience from the week and tell me about it.
7 How did the artmaking (prompting: video, writing, etc.) challenge you to think about the Civil Rights movement? Probing may include:

   a What is something you learned about the Civil Rights movement
   b What is something that surprised you?
   c Think about a specific experience and tell me about it.

8 Think of one place we visited that you remember the most. How did being there challenge you to think differently? Probing may include:

   a Tell me about the place and what you remember.
   b Was it different than what you expected?
   c What was important about being there?
   d What did you learn that you wouldn't have if you hadn't been there?

9 What would be the best way for teachers to use this approach in their classrooms?
10 What do you hope other young people learn from this curriculum?
11 What would you want to do differently if you got to do it all over again?
12 What is something that surprised you this week?

At the closing of the week, we asked students to complete an artist statement worksheet. Once the week concluded, the teacher/researchers all worked together to create a plan for an exhibition on campus, where we asked students and their families to return and view all of their work professionally displayed in one of our galleries. During this closing exhibition, students were given the opportunity to share with their peers, families, and friends anything they wanted about their artwork or the week. All of the teens returned to campus with their families to participate in the closing reception, an event that brought all of the work to a close.

Conclusion

While we hope this weekly overview gives a clear idea of how we engaged in this project, we also understand that there are limitations in both time and resources in more traditional education environments. So, while we were fortunate to have a large pool of resources in Tallahassee and at Florida State University, we know this is not the same at other institutions and schools. To support other teachers in their work to design, develop, and implement strategies for inspiring civic participation and engagement through the arts, we spend much of the final section of the book offering recommendations and suggestions for practicing teachers. The next section, however, spends time unpacking how positioning students as researchers in an art classroom gives them space to deeply engage in the explorations of local people, places, and events. Chapters 7 through 9 are organized around people, places, and events, with each chapter taking the reader through two illustrative case studies. These cases are written from the perspective of the teacher/researchers and rely heavily on the words and reflections of the teens. We present the teens' artistic research processes through our lens as art educators, calling upon our personal repertoire of educational and artistic experiences. Occasionally these narratives also offer sections titled *historical notes* and *resonance*. These sections offer contextualizing information in a way that is intended to expand the readers' understanding of the students' work. We felt it was important for the reader to have relevant historical information, allowing for a more holistic understanding of the individual student's inquiry processes and artistic interpretations. The sections titled *resonance* offer a researcher reflection and analysis and each case study closes with a section where we make connections between thinking, making, and acting.

These individual case studies are organized around people, places, and events and unpack how each student was engaged in thinking, making, and acting in their individual art exploration. It is important to note that these artistic processes are not independent of one another and did not occur linearly. While we present these narratives in a linear, time-bound format, the work the students started, stopped, and stalled to varying degrees. We hope these cases will provide the reader with an understanding of how students engaged in arts-based research and paint a portrait of how these young people began to see themselves and each other as change makers.

Reference

Faber, S. (2019). *"A photograph doesn't lie": Ricard Martínez & Susanna Muriel on re-photography and the Spanish Civil War*. The Volunteer. https://albavolunteer.org/2019/08/a-photograph-doesnt-lie-re-photography-and-the-spanish-civil-war/

Section III
Make

6   Engaging People

In this chapter, we look to the fields of social studies and art education by positioning the specific curricular strategies of first-person narratives and portraiture together in a way that engages teens in an arts-based exploration of local history and historical figures. The cases in the chapter feature the work of two high school students. The first, Iyawa, who attended in the summer of 2018 and 2019. Both summers she explored the history of the civil rights movement through detailed linocut prints. Her prints responded to first-person accounts of individuals who participated in the movement, and her printmaking style and process developed over the course of the two summers. This extended participation resulted in the completion of a large body of work that paid homage to the young bodies that both won and were lost in the pursuit of civil rights. The second, Dwayne, attended in the summer of 2019. He joined us just after graduating from a local high school and spent the week exploring the lives of three Black men whose experiences track the fight for civil rights from the past into the present day. Dwayne was inspired by Iyawa's printmaking, and despite never working in the medium, he created a triptych of prints honoring the lives and legacies of each man.

We have paired these two cases together because they both used the process of making portraits to come to know their city, their history, and ultimately themselves. Through the research and the artistic skill of paying attention to detail, Iyawa and Dwayne found their own ways to bear witness to history, using their research and artmaking processes to humanize and render themselves visible inside historical narratives. We close this chapter by speculating on the ways that seeing and recognizing oneself in history holds potential for expanding possibilities for both civic and art education (Gude, 2004). In doing this, we reflect on what implications for future civic engagement and learning might result from

DOI: 10.4324/9781003199106-9

participation in this program, and specifically in relation to the focus on people while doing history.

Iyawa's portraits of the past

Iyawa was one of four participants who completed both the 2018 and 2019 summer programs, when she was a rising junior and a rising senior, respectively. She attended a Title 1 High School with a majority Black student population inside Tallahassee's city limits. In Spring of 2018, Iyawa was nominated by her school guidance counselor to attend the program. Between 2018 and 2019, she kept in touch with us by attending a series of workshops we organized during the school year, and enthusiastically accepted our invitation to return for the summer of 2019. At the start of the first year, in an early field guide entry, Iyawa filled out a page that prompted her to reflect on what she knew about the civil rights movement. Her response was comprehensive, citing Martin Luther King, Jr., Rosa Parks, and Malcom X, along with noting the use of police brutality and the centrality of voting rights. She was the only student in 2018 who demonstrated local knowledge of the civil rights movement by citing the success of the Tallahassee bus boycott. Just like her, her notes are neat and factual. Iyawa was meticulous, she thought about every step in the process. As we flipped through the field guide pages, revisited transcripts, and looked at process photos, you could almost recreate her thoughts, reflections, and artistic choices (see Figure 6.1). We came to know Iyawa as a thoughtful and insightful young person with a highly proficient and visually striking artistic style.

One week prior to the inauguration of the 2018 summer program, the Emmett Till murder investigation was re-opened by the United States Department of Justice. We debated for days about whether to include the news footage of the Emmett Till's investigation. These were kids after all, what would showing the video accomplish? We worried that the violence would come too close to home, as these kids were just teenagers, and many of them Black, just like Emmett Till. Ultimately, we decided that we wanted students to see that the civil rights movement was not just a movement about racism, but was an eruption of change that was predicated by decades deeply disturbing narratives braided together to form collective experience. But more importantly, inside of this collective experience are thousands of individual stories, many about young people, that have never been heard. We made the decision to start by hearing Emmett Till's story, as a reminder that stories matter and that there are thousands more stories about everyday people that no one has ever heard. Together we committed to spending the week remembering these people and their stories.

Figure 6.1 Documentation of Iyawa's portraits of the past

Historical note

Emmett Till, a 14 year old Black boy from Chicago, was visiting his uncle in Mississippi, when he went to the grocery store to buy gum. Till was said to be seen talking or whistling at the White cashier. Though reports remain unclear, the cashier said in a 2017 interview that Till had done nothing inappropriate. Later that day, the cashier's husband and brother drove to Emmett Till's uncle's house and at gunpoint demanded to see him. They took him from his uncle and he was never seen again. His body was found in a lake 3 days later, severely beaten and weighted down with barbed wire tied to a cotton-gin fan. The two men were arrested, tried, and found not-guilty after only an hour of deliberation by the all White jury. Till's mother, in an effort to highlight their brutality, held an open casket funeral where Jet Magazine was allowed to photograph and publish images of Emmett Till's battered body. Historians speculate that Till's death marked the beginning of the modern civil rights movement.

(Hudson-Weems, 1998)

After watching the documentary on the Till case, we asked students to reflect on the civil rights movement and how Emmett Till's murder, and his mother's decision to publish images of his body, pushed the civil rights movement into the national spotlight. Iyawa captured her response on a page of the field guide, writing, "I can really feel the hate because they actually killed him for no reason ... It really shows me how evil people can really be." This commentary shows a shift from the listing of facts and names related to bus boycotts, toward a more emotional response to this historic moment, as she reflected on injustice and hate. For Iyawa, this sensitivity to first-person narratives became a driving force behind her artmaking, providing a powerful entry point for reflecting on and responding to the historical weight of the civil rights movement and giving us insight into the rich nature of people-first approaches to historical research.

In 2018, Iyawa began that first week by identifying case files to research; she selected Clement Carney, John Broxton, Willie Larkins, Angela Narice, and Barbara Broxton—all participants in the Tallahassee Woolworth lunch counter sit-ins. We visited the state archives and dove into the file folders, where she spent the entire time tracing down the individuals from her case files. In the notes she took during her early investigation of her case files, she cited well-known facts, "arrested for sit ins at lunch counters, refusing to post bail, Reverend C.K. Steele, Henry Steele." Half-way through the morning, we saw her pouring over a new folder and notice she deviated from the sit-ins. She shared with the group that she found documentation of the 1964 Tampa Riots. Later, when preparing an initial draft of her final project, she wrote about images documenting both the race riots in Florida and reactionary measures taken by state law enforcement encouraging police to limit the congregation of Black people. In her field guide, she jotted down the following "Something that has to do with the riots that show people unrest; Vandalism; Fire bombs; Rocks thrown; Telephone damage; Bottle burning; Looting in stores; Tampa riots 1964; Group of Blacks standing around doing nothing cops walking by looking suspiciously; Medium: charcoal, graphite, pen."

Despite starting with a case file, Iyawa, like many others in the group, became fixated on events. This was particularly true after the visit to the state archive, where the group spent a lot of time talking about and sharing police reports and memos from the governor. There was collective disbelief in how comfortable the government and law enforcement were with racist language and rhetoric. By giving students first-hand accounts of events, the archives did a lot to bring history to life. Acknowledging the importance of these moments, we left the state archives and returned to campus to try and bring the archives to life. In an attempt to bring first-hand written accounts into the present, we set up a face-to-face conversation with Rev. Henry Steele, son of Rev. C. K. Steele, to discuss his choices and the experience of being an activist as a teenager.

Historical note

Rev. C. K. Steele was pastor at Bethel Baptist Church in Tallahassee, he was also a pillar of the civil rights movement locally and nationally. He served as the head of the local National Association for the Advancement of Colored People chapter, as the first vice president of the Southern Christian Leadership Conference, and as president of the Inter-Civic Council. In 1956, Henry Steele, his son, watched his father organize one of only two successful bus boycotts in the country. His father's activism had long-standing impacts on his family. The Steele family hosted Martin Luther King, Jr. in their home during one of his visits to Tallahassee. They also experienced many aggressive and violent acts of vandalism. Still, despite the danger to himself and his family, Henry Steele made the decision to commit to the movement through non-violent means.

At the age of 16, Steele participated in the Woolworth's lunch counter sit-ins in Tallahassee. He was subsequently arrested for his participation and made history as one the first group of people to choose jail over bail as a form of peaceful protest, and also the first high school student to do so.

(Stanford University King Papers, 2016)

As we listened to Rev. Henry Steele's story, we looked around the room and saw fixed stares and mouths agape. The teens were enthralled with him, they asked questions, listened attentively, took notes, and by the end of his visit you could feel the energy in the room shifting. Listening to Henry Steele recount his experience as a teenager protesting, serving jail time, and even working on a chain gang gave the historical movement we discovered in the archives a name and face. His story had a deep impact on the students, and Iyawa's artwork and reflections mirror the attentiveness of the group as a whole. In her exit interview, she recalled listening and responding to Steele's story:

He's been done wrong his whole life so he was fearless when he was at the counter, because he was tired of being done wrong his whole life. And then my project is of the man, and he's like, looks tired, and he's tired of everything that's been going on, like, all the wrong that's been done to him.

As Iyawa began to hone in on her glowing data (MacLure, 2010, 2020), it became apparent that the case files and police reports from the early days of our project were no longer in the forefront of her mind. Despite her early plans to depict scenes of vandalism or directly reference images from the Tampa race riots, she chose to focus on the personal narrative of Henry Steele. In her field guide she reflected on the emotional impact of racism, and her work showed feelings of weight, history, and tiredness. Her second set of planning notes included the following:

Printmaking/John Michel Basquiat; Henry Steele: he was fearless, I've been done wrong my whole life; Black/white/orange/charcoal; Print of a face; Marks on face like my grandma; Youraba [sic] marks; Mandingo/Mandinka; A woman in a tribal print with a baby on her back in modern day America.

(Iyawa's Field Guide; see Figure 6.1)

In her planning notes we also see a collision of past and present, personal and shared, local and global. We observed how Iyawa began to formulate a project making visual references to Basquiat, a Black artist she recognized as an advocate for the Black community. We also see reference to the tribal markings her grandmother had. In these few notes, you start to see her micro and macro worlds collide. She was floating somewhere between Henry Steele's experience and her own, between material processes and contemporary artists. In the same notes where she identified Basquiat as impactful, she wrote "printmaking" (see Figure 6.1). Interspersed with her written reflections, Iyawa spent time drawing a man's face, a face that she later reproduced. Iyawa chose to work with printmaking, a rigid and unforgiving approach to portraiture. She juxtaposed that style with textured, vibrant brush work on the paper she later mounted the prints on. We were curious about this shift to printmaking, especially after she shared with us her initial interest in drawing. Below you see where she uses the field guide to recount an interaction about these decisions after having a conversation with one of the graduate student instructors, Danielle:

> I chose printmaking because Danielle said that my drawing style was like it, and then also it gives you like the torn down vibe, like it's really old.

Here again, a reference to the then, via her interest in a "torn down vibe like it's really old," and the now, from earlier in her field guide where she planned using the bright colored paint smears that mimicked the work of Basquiat. Once at work, her process was repetitive, pulling print after print, arranging the portrait across contrasting backgrounds, trying different backgrounds and different inks. For a full day, we watched her experiment with the possibilities of printmaking as she explored printing and cutting out the prints, printing directly on the background, painting over and under. She worked fast, almost frenzied, and as the prints stacked up, we saw her individual portrait transform into a collective gaze, capturing an experience of tiredness and fearlessness that was reiterated, over and over again. This process reappeared in her second summer with us. While the people of the past were the focus of her work during the summer of 2018, the people of the present and potential of the future became her focus during the summer of 2019.

Iyawa began the summer of 2019 with Black Lives Matter on her mind. In a field guide prompt that asked her to describe a social justice issue she cared about, she wrote: "BLM, Say Her Name, Sandra Bland, Do Black Lives Matter to You" (see Figure 6.1). That day, she made stickers and a digital poster with the Black Lives Matter slogan. Her poster used images of her prints from the year before, and under the title "The New Jim Crow," she included data about the incarceration rate of people of color, and of Black men specifically (see Figure 6.1). This early research is clearly built out of her prior summer engagement, hinting at the long-standing impact of this work on her. At some point (we speculate it was while she was collecting data for her poster), Iyawa read an article about the execution of George Stinney, Jr., who was sentenced to death by the state of South Carolina in 1944. He was cruelly placed in an electric chair at the age of 14; Iyawa was 17. In her 2019 field guide, she described her process and provided context:

> My pieces are prints of the silhouette of George Stinney Jr. [sic] head using a picture of one of his mugshots. The print method I used was linocut printmaking. I was inspired to make this piece because of a [sic] article I saw online about George Stinney Jr.'s execution at age 14. He was not allowed a fair trial with the all White jury deciding his fate in only 10 minutes.
>
> (Iyawa's Field Guide; see Figure 6.1)

Historical note

In March 1944, deep in the Jim Crow South, police came for 14-year-old George Stinney, Jr. His parents weren't at home. His little sister was hiding in the family's chicken coop behind the house in Alcolu, a segregated mill town in South Carolina, while officers handcuffed George and his older brother, Johnnie, and took them away. Two young White girls had been found brutally murdered, beaten over the head with a railroad spike and dumped in a water-logged ditch. George and his little sister, who were Black, were said to be the last people to see them alive. Authorities later released the older Stinney brother—and directed their attention toward George ... He was questioned in a small room, alone—without his parents, without an attorney ... Police claimed the boy confessed ... After a two-hour trial and a 10-minute jury deliberation, Stinney was convicted of murder on April 24 and sentenced to die by electrocution ... Indeed, just 84 days after the girls' deaths, Stinney was sent to the electric chair ... Stinney was barely 5 feet tall and not yet 100 pounds. The electric chair's straps were too big for his frail body. Newspapers at the time reported he had to sit on books to reach the headpiece.

(Bever, 2014, n.p.)

As you look across Iyawa's artwork, field guide, and reflections, you see echoes of Emmett Till and repetitions of printing Henry Steele's face, clear nods to the previous year's work. Like in 2018, Iyawa built her project around an individual's portrait, yet this time, the person had a name and a fixed identity. She chose to create a larger-than-life-size linocut. At around 20 inches tall, the visual is powerful to see in person. Like her printing process from the year before, she multiplied the portrait of George Sinney, Jr. through a series of prints, again placing sets of black and white prints over swaths of bright, contrasting strokes of paint (see Figure 6.1). The work is striking, resonant, and impactful. One piece has the number 14, in reference to George Stinney, Jr.'s age, written under each printed portrait, underneath that she wrote the word "execution." Toward the end of the week, Iyawa jotted down several affirming project updates in her field guide:

> I love my artwork and also the message and idea behind it, which is George Stinney.

> The boldness of my print is really working, it really stands out.

The interplay between message and material is a focus that emerged the year prior, and continued to inform Iyawa's artistic choices. In her second year of the program, Iyawa revisted a question from the year before: how does one make art that communicates the emotional impact of the Black struggle? Iyawa maintained her interest in the relationship between her material choices and the message she was trying to convey. In her exit interview in 2019, she reflected on her project:

> Mine is based off the Black struggle and I like the printmaking style, cuz you look at printmaking, or at least the ones I make, it looks like it's been through some stuff you know? And that's what I like about that, and that's, like, a conscious decision … With art, I mean you want it to look good and you also, you want to convey a message, and you want it to all come together and it's really hard! So like, it just makes me think a lot more and put more care into the art.

Resonance

As we reflect on Iyawa's experience, we see the possibilities that recurring investigations hold for students. When young people have the opportunity to have sustained engagement into a research process, it gives them the chance to stretch out and spend time in the process of thinking and making. As teachers we are often rushing students onto the next thing, and we run the risk of missing ideas yet to be realized. Iyawa's experience is a powerful example of the importance of time and focus. She spent much of the first summer grappling with the personal narrative of Rev. Henry Steele, but ultimately chose to depict a nameless man. She researched deeply the police brutality of the Tampa Riots, but only included small nods and references to these in one of the many pieces she created. While she printed her pieces in the first summer, she was consumed with visual decision making, the colors, the backgrounds, the printing surface. While we observed a deep resonance with the words of Henry Steele in conversation and in her field guide, little of that made its way into her pieces.

Between the first and second summers, Iyawa, along with a few other students, continued to meet with us on the weekends, where we gathered together a few times a month to continue our conversations and artmaking from the summer. These conversations were focused on the present and future, asking questions like, what now? And, how can we share what we've learned with others? When she rejoined us in the second summer she hit the ground running, spending two days exploring and creating artwork about the Black Lives Matter movement. On the second or third day she discovered George Stinney, Jr.'s story, she saw his face, and in it, she recognized something familiar, a life that matters. She dedicated the last three days of the week to the creation of his portrait, printing his likeness over and over and over. The catharsis of this seems obvious as we revisit the work, her notes, and the closing interview. During this interview, she reflected:

> I would say that's what kind of surprised me, but then not really, because like people go unnoticed everyday.

Her mentioning of the unnoticed felt significant; was her work an act of recognizing, remembering, and honoring? We return to her interest in the Black Lives Matter movement from the second week, knowing this movement is about recognizing, remembering, and honoring Black lives as precious. We asked Iyawa about her interest in the Black Lives Matter movement, having already shared with us her distrust and disappointment in the ways her school had avoided discussion around this movement. She responded:

> I think that would have been like the most important thing for me.... Cuz they [BLM] stood on a lot of points that really hit, especially like if you have an idea [just] start something. If you want to make a change, do it ... that got me really excited.

We saw this excitement in her work, in the juxtaposition of bright colors with somber, even sad, portraits. Her work from both summers hinted at the complicatedness of contemporary struggles for civil rights, and how the powerful combination of voices across the country often doesn't happen until lives are lost. We see the frustration of arguing that Black Lives Matter, in a nation that responds with the call of All Lives Matter. We see the solidarity of thousands of people coming together around a movement, laced with the sorrow that we still must fight this fight. But in all this messiness, we also see hope for the future of our country, we see a life that matters deeply and a future that holds potential for change.

Dwayne's triptych

Dwayne was an attendee at our 2019 summer art intensive. He came to us from a Title 1 high school that historically performs under the county and state test score averages in all subjects except history. Dwayne was recommended for the program by his art teacher who stated in his nomination packet, "Dwayne loves drawing, is motivated, and a hard worker." Dwayne was our only teen participant that was over the age of 18 and had recently graduated high school. He rode the city bus to and from campus every day to attend. As a participant he was highly motivated and deeply invested in learning about this history of civil rights, he found deep resonance with the stories of the young people that contributed to the movement, remarking often about how they were so close in age. On the first day, Dwayne spent an extended period of time finding the case file he wanted to work through, eventually selecting the file for George Calvin Bess, Jr. Later in the week when the women who participated in the first Woolworth sit-ins visited with us, they asked the students to share who they had chosen for their case file. Below is an exchange between them and Dwayne.

Dwayne: I chose my foot solider cause how old he was when he was murdered. Calvin Bess. And that's like—I have three years to be that age, so that really struck me.

Gloria: Now, let me tell you the story about Calvin Bess. Calvin Bess was a student at FAMU and Calvin Bess had gone to Mississippi to help with the voting rights. Well, Calvin Bess is from the community right here in Tallahassee, the community on the other side of FAMU. I met his mother and his father. Calvin was killed back in Mississippi back in the early 60s. Calvin's murderer has never been found. His face is still out there. His sister is still on the internet, begging people, "please, we've got to bring some closure to his case." You have a very interesting choice in him cause Calvin's case is out there. They said Calvin had drown and the family knew he was murdered. Calvin was a student at FAMU and, of course, he went to Mississippi to help with the voting but never came back home. Went through the training and everything, but never came back home. His mother died of a broken heart. She was never able to—I knew his mother and his father and she died of a broken heart cause she never got peace with her son's death.

Historical note

George Calvin Bess, Jr. was 22 when they found his body and car in a creek off the side of a road in Mississippi, it was the summer of 1967. I'm sure that summer was sticky, as southern summers are, when he climbed into his new blue Cadillac and left Tallahassee to register voters in Selma. Somewhere along the way Calvin changed his plans and called to tell his parents that he was going to Mississippi instead, his father replied, "well you're in no-man's land now" (see Due & Due, 2009). The next time they heard from Mississippi, it was the sheriff calling to tell them that Calvin was dead. His death remains mysterious, with the report noting only a head injury and abandoned car. No one believed the police report, and the fear of a similar fate kept everyone away from the truth. Today, Calvin's death is listed as suspicious in the state archives.

Sitting down next to Dwayne, we asked if he had found anything in the archives. He shuffled through some papers and pulled out a pamphlet with red and black stripes with stars at the top, one star was colored red (see Figure 6.2). We looked together, shocked by the "triple murder" headline that others of the dangers encountered when registering voters. Dwayne wondered if Calvin might have seen this when he was only 21, not knowing the fate that awaited him. Dwayne was quiet, eventually remarking that he was 18. This moment was critical for Dwayne, as he sat in the archives and filed through the notes from his morning, we can only imagine that he recognized himself. Though the archives were empty of any real reference to Calvin Bess, Dwayne did not give up. As he Googled his way to the whole story he found Tananarive and Patricia Stephens Due's book (Due & Due, 2009), blogs, and other bread-crumb trails that mentioned Calvin's life and legacy. As he continued his search, Dwayne began to research other Black men, like John Africa and Michael Brown, who were stolen from their families and whose stories were distorted or misreported in official reports.

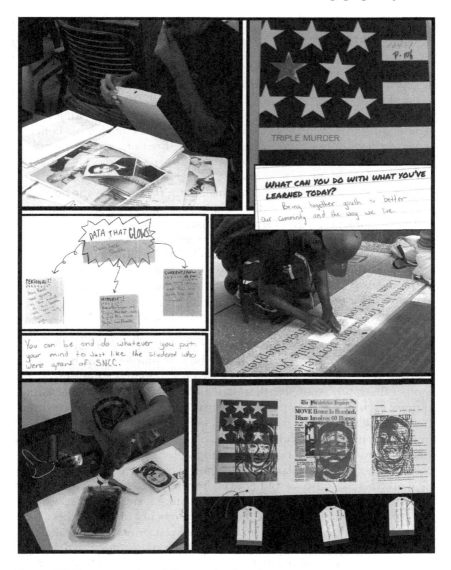

Figure 6.2 Documentation of Dwayne's triptych

Historical note

John Africa was a Black activist and father, whose life was stolen in 1985. John was the founder of MOVE, a Philadelphia-based, predominantly black organization in the early 1970s. He, and several members and their children, were inside a residential building that served as the movement's headquarters, when the Philadelphia Police Department bombed the house and let the fire burn out of control. While the building burned, the people inside faced the impossible choice of dying inside from the fire or trying to escape and dying in the firefight right outside the basement door; the next day the burned remains of five children and six adults were recovered (Washington, 1989). Unlike John and Calvin, Michael Brown was not a part of a movement, but instead started a movement. Michael Brown, an 18 year old Black boy, was shot and killed by Ferguson police during an altercation. While the police were never accused of his murder, the incident spurred both peaceful and violent protests across the country (Mourão et al., 2021).

As Dwayne worked you could see him piecing together a narrative held together by stories about a Black boy who was murdered for believing in a movement, a Black man who was killed for founding a movement, and another Black boy whose death started a movement. He told us he wanted to draw each of them, but when he began this task he became frustrated that he couldn't capture their likeness, seemingly worried that he wasn't doing them justice. We showed him how to use photoshop to exaggerate shadows and create shapes in the photographs, then how to use the projector to trace the shapes and create a positive/negative image of the face. He worked close to Iyawa and noticed how her prints captured just black and white and he asked if he could try creating a small print of Calvin's portrait. In the next two days, he created linocuts of Calvin Bess, then John Africa, then Michael Brown. He pulled test prints as he struggled to decide what to print on (see Figure 6.2). He experimented with colored paper, white paper, and painted paper similar to Iyawa's. On the last day he asked if he could print out images that corresponded with each of the men. For Calvin Bess, the triple murder pamphlet he found in the archives, for John Africa, the newspaper article documenting the bombing, and for Michael Brown, a screenshot of a Google search of his case yielding about 1,130,000,000 results.

He went on to print their faces on these documents, using red, black, and blue ink, a clear nod to the threat of being Black in America (see

Figure 6.2). Danielle introduced the idea of a triptych, "a picture or relief carving on three panels, typically hinged together side by side and used as an altarpiece" (Oxford English Dictionary, n.d., n.p.). In the final rush of the last day, he decided to hang tags at the bottom of each image, alluding to the toe tags hung on bodies in a morgue (see Figure 6.2). This flurry of activity went up to the second we released the teens to go home. His artist statement remained unfinished, because instead of telling us what his piece was about, he finished his altarpiece, titling it *Triple Murder*, a clear reference to the pamphlet he found on the first day in the state archives. In his field guide we found the abandoned artist statement where he wrote:

> My piece is pointing a spotlight on the wrongful murders of three African-American men through the years. I was inspired by the murder case of Calvin Bess and how his murder was unsolved. There was a little trouble with the craving [sic] of Mike Brown. The reason I chose this topic was how ....

Resonance

In Dwayne's exit interview he told us, "there's more detail about what we learned in the school system, there's more to the story." These forgotten and overlooked details became the focus of his research, and while he used their faces in his final piece, he returned to the ways their lives paralleled his. Calvin Bess, representing a version of Dwayne in the not-too-distant future, John Africa, the father Dwayne might become, and Michael Brown, the friend Dwayne could have had. Dwayne's story has stayed with us. We remember listening to him in the exit interview, feeling overwhelming heartache. Today we ask ourselves, was this a projection of our own identities as mothers of small children, thinking about how little time Calvin Bess had with his own mother, or was this us witnessing Dwayne's act of recognition? Perhaps it was both. Whatever the reality, this recognition is what is important about working with the stories of people. The stories of people's lives give us access points to empathetic understanding, and deepen our capacity to sit in the spaces others occupy. The stories of people invite us in and remind us of our own experiences. In these moments of deep reflection, we catch glimpses of the familiar, we see ourselves, as Dwayne did in Calvin and Michael, and we wonder what it must have felt like. We hope, like Dwayne commented, that we might "[try] to figure out what happened to these people ... [to be able to let] the families and relatives know what happened to these people."

Perhaps Dwayne's work did more than memorialize the lives of three Black men. Perhaps the process of drawing, printing, and assembling the portrait triptych gave Dwayne an opportunity to create a place to return to, an altar to highlight the preciousness of life, where he could recognize himself in the stories of others, and move forward in ways that honor those that have come before him. The people Dwayne depicted in his work were foundational to the research and creative process, as he responded to and engaged with the proximity of their lives to his. When we asked Dwayne what surprised him from the week he said, "I don't think anything really surprised me. Growing up, this wasn't a secret or anything." In the process of humanizing the stories of Black lives stolen too soon, we see the precarity of Dwayne's own story, and we can't help but feel our own connection to him. As teachers do, we often wonder where these kids are now, what they are doing, and how this work impacted them. But then we remember that maybe that is the beauty of this kind of people-oriented arts-driven inquiry into local histories, it provides openings for young people to tell their own stories, write their own histories, and leave their own breadcrumbs. Dwayne reminded us that these experiences are what inspire us to look into the faces of our students and recognize students from years before and years yet to come. For Dwayne, and for us, this recognition allows us to bear witness to the present, while looking for glimpses of the familiar and whispers of the past, all while doing the work of creating portraits of the future.

Conclusion

As I once suggested in an inaugural lecture on "History as Imagination," we must employ our imaginative faculties throughout the historical process because, as Logan Pearsall Smith once wrote to Virginia Woolf, "People only exist for us in our thoughts about them. They float like slow, strange fish in the ... aquarium tanks of our imaginations." One of our obligations is to ensure that our conceptions of those strange "others," especially past ones, approximate as closely as possible the rounded reality and self-image of the others themselves. But since we gain access to past people only through the piecemeal evidence they have left, we must use our imaginations to reanimate the known facts and restore them to life, to fill the holes in our evidence with informed guesses, to reestablish, in the face of hindsight's certainties, the choices that the dead once enjoyed in the past, and to discern the larger forces that transcended and patterned the individual lives of our subjects.

(Axtell, 1998, p. 436)

An imaginative approach to learning is not relegated just to the study of history. Art and art education also have a deep relationship with imagination. Greene (2000) writes on the social imagination as a bridge between the past and present. In her essays, she uses art that speaks to historical events, often traumatic ones, to illustrate the possibilities for the arts to awaken an imaginative re-envisioning of the present and future. She sees social imagination as a way to "invent visions of what should be and what might be" (Greene, 2000, p. 5). Greene believed the role of imagination in schools was to move toward action and transformation. This is supported by the cases of Iyawa and Dwayne, where we found that when encouraged to think and make like historians and artists, empathy, transformation, and agency emerged (Waldron et al., 2021). These characteristics are future-oriented, as they ask students to interrogate narratives, understand perspectives, and ultimately bring person-first historical stories into their own lives and think differently about their future. Through the use of first-person investigations, we found Iyawa and Dwayne were able to identify themselves in historical narratives (think), begin to witness and remember historical figures (make), and ultimately see themselves as agential beings capable of impacting the local histories unfolding around them (act).

Thinking, making, and acting with people

We close this chapter with an exploration of the artistic process of portraiture and discuss how it might also be a way of bearing witness and humanizing history. In this closing discussion, we speculate on the ways that seeing and recognizing oneself in history hold potential for expanding the possibilities for both civic and art education (Gude, 2004). In doing this, we reflect on what implications for future civic engagement and learning might result from participation in this program, and in relation to the focus on people as history.

People form the foundation of history, meaning not one person or perspective creates a historical moment, but rather the convergence of multiple, differing, and often conflicting personal experiences creates a vision of history that is as multifaceted as the world we live in. When approaching learning from a person first perspective, we asked young people to position themselves as local historians and arts-based researchers, doing history and art through their investigation of the lived experience of individuals in their city's history. Looking closely, we saw how first-person perspectives engaged Iyawa and Dwayne in a negotiation of the ways that people, and their decision making, are the foundation for historical events.

As Iyawa and Dwayne researched lived experiences, they worked toward a representation of history that was not a victor's history, but a people's history. When history becomes about people, their choices, and the outcomes of those choices, young people can begin to see how they might contribute to their own community's history in the making. Central to the Foot Soldier program's curriculum was how we asked teens to select individuals to research, while also discussing the centrality of people as embedded in and working for the rights of communities. This shifting of historical narratives away from stagnant events from decades past, into the active cause and effects of real people making everyday decisions, asked students to engage in introspective inquiry focused on their own lives, communities, and decision making practices. Specifically, by examining "how human decision making is implicated in present-day problems of distribution and sustainability and help them to conceptualise themselves as agentic in the face of seemingly intractable problems" (Waldron et al., 2021, p. 26).

This approach to doing history and artistic inquiry stands in contrast to a version of learning seen across many subject areas, where the curriculum is broken up into themes and the teacher illustrates or demonstrates the main ideas for students. This is an approach that "is unlikely to cultivate the habits of mind associated with active citizenship and liberal learning" (Sipress & Voelker, 2009, p. 21). Instead, we see potential in a version of teaching and learning that centers the imagination of the student, as they inquire into a topic, idea, or in the case of this chapter, a person.

References

Axtell, J. (1998). Encountering the other. In J. Axtell (Ed.), *The pleasures of academe* (pp. 69–84). University of Nebraska Press.

Bever, L. (2014, December 18). It took 10 minutes to convict 14-year-old George Stinney Jr. It took 70 years after his execution to exonerate him. *The Washington Post*. https://www.washingtonpost.com/news/morning-mix/wp/2014/12/18/the-rush-job-conviction-of-14-year-old-george-stinney-exonerated-70-years-after-execution/

Due, T., & Due, P. S. (2009). *Freedom in the family: A mother-daughter memoir of the fight for civil rights*. One World.

Greene, M. (2000). *Releasing the imagination: Essays on education, the arts, and social change*. John Wiley & Sons.

Gude, O. (2004). Postmodern principles: In search of a 21st century art education. *Art Education*, 57(1), 6–14. https://doi.org/10.1080/00043125.2004.11653528

Hudson-Weems, C. (1998). Resurrecting Emmett Till: The catalyst of The modern civil rights movement. *Journal of Black Studies*, 29(2), 179–188. https://doi.org/10.1177/002193479802900203

MacLure, M. (2010). The offence of theory. *Journal of Education Policy*, 25(2), 275–283. https://doi.org/10.1080/02680930903462316

MacLure, M. (2020). Inquiry as divination. *Qualitative Inquiry*, 23(4), 345–370. https://doi.org/10.1177/1077800420939124

Mourão, R. R., Brown, D. K., & Sylvie, G. (2021). Framing Ferguson: The interplay of advocacy and journalistic frames in local and national newspaper coverage of Michael Brown. *Journalism*, 22(2), 320–340. https://doi.org/10.1177/1464884918778722

Oxford English Dictionary. (n.d.). *Triptych*. Oxford University Press. https://www.oed.com/view/Entry/206357?redirectedFrom=triptych#eid

Sipress, J. M., & Voelker, D. J. (2009). From learning history to doing history. In R. A. R. Gurung, N. L. Chick, & A. Haynie (Eds.), *Exploring signature pedagogies: Approaches to teaching disciplinary habits of mind* (pp. 19–35). Stylus Publishing.

Stanford University King Papers. (2016). To C. Kenzie Steele. The Martin Luther King, Jr., Research and Education Institute. https://kinginstitute.stanford.edu/king-papers/documents/c-kenzie-steele-0

Waldron, F., Cassaithe, C. N., Barry, M., & Whelan, P. (2021). Critical historical enquiry for a socially just and sustainable world. In, A. M. Kavanagh, F. Waldron, & B. Mallon (Eds.), *Teaching for social justice and sustainable development across the primary curriculum* (pp. 21–36). Routledge. https://doi.org/10.4324/9781003003021

Washington, L. (1989). MOVE: Double standard of justice. *Yale Journal of Law and Liberation, 1,* 67–82.

7 Visiting Places

Place is intertwined in our experiences of learning. Young people learn in schools, families, neighborhoods, and as residents of communities, churches, states, and nations. Our worlds are made up of places of learning, where education is at once formal, in terms of schooling, and informal, in terms of socialization. Places themselves can also be educational, popping up in textbooks or serving as a destination for field trips. Landmarks, historic sites, monuments, and cultural heritage markers are physical reminders of history, connecting the past to an unfolding present. When considering the role of place in an arts-informed approach to civics, we find that both social spaces and local places have a role in activating young people's engagement with their past, their community, and their collective future. The following cases explore what civic learning students can engage in when thinking, making and acting with or within places. They illuminate the ways in which local places might support civic education, reflecting on the interplay between place, civics and learning through artmaking. We will focus on the processes of Theo, Zoe, and Viola, as we explore the complexity of place as a material that holds history. The cases look at how the act of visiting places and experiencing learning in places other than classrooms offers ways for young people to see their communities differently. They allow us to consider how being in historic sites, visiting archives, or even being in the relational space of social movements, presented opportunities for different layers of place to inform students' positioning as civic participants. Throughout the chapter, we elaborate on a situated understanding of a civic engagement environment that is informed by the past, grounded in localities, and activated within the vibrant social space of communities.

Theo and Zoe walking and collaborating

In 2018, Theo was a rising 8th grader at a middle school on the northside of Tallahassee that consistently ranks as the top middle school in the city. Theo was recommended for the program by his guidance counselor

DOI: 10.4324/9781003199106-10

because he was "well-mannered and worked hard." Zoe was a freshman at a local Christian private school that also ranks as one of the top private schools in the area. Theo and Zoe became friends during our 2018 program, where they walked to and from all of the site visits together. On the last day, when the teens were asked to pair up to reflect on the week, Theo and Zoe elected to meet with us together. In the exit interviews, Theo and Zoe emphasized the walks. As we recapped the week, we asked what stood out to them, and Zoe responded with one word: walking. Theo chimed in saying, "I was 'bout to say yeah, that was fun. We were able to walk with each other and just talk. And then once we get to the place you know...," Zoe finished his thought saying, "It's like, you're tired then you're like whoa, look at all this stuff. It was..." Theo interrupted, "It was pretty cool. Cause I mean, you're going around town and I mean like you can, like wherever you are, I mean, you can see different things, and like, you know you have your friends by you and you can talk to them and stuff." Zoe continued, "Yeah ... It was like, if we were just taking a car or something, it would be different. Cause like, we were walking, exercising, and like talking, and like seeing it through like, not a [car] window but, through your eyes. It was, yeah ..." Theo finished her thought, "Like, really experiencing. You know what foot soldiers [were] experiencing. Actually walking and not riding around everywhere ... Like, just do[ing] what they usually did back in the day, walk everywhere."

In our exit interviews, every one of the teens in the first summer session spoke about the significance of walking. While this was an outcome we had hoped for, the combination of the summer heat and blaring sun left us wondering if the walks would be impactful at all. Summer weather in this city is extreme, and the experience of walking the city with teens was heavy with both humidity and history. With an average temperature in the high 90s, we departed campus with our water bottles full, our Foot Soldiers hats pulled down, and sweat beading on our foreheads. At first, the invitation to walk in the summertime was met with groans from students as they filed down the sidewalk, interrupted only occasionally by the whoosh of traffic. As a commuter city, Tallahassee is mostly empty of pedestrians, instead filled with cars zipping from one side of town to another. Once you leave the institutional safety of the city's two large campuses, with their blinking crosswalks and labeled buildings, the sidewalks remain relatively vacant. As we marched down the road, we traced the route laid out in our field guides that took us from a church, to a bus station, to a monument, and ending at the state archives.

Both Zoe and Theo used these places as the impetus for their art-making. As they circulated the city, the places that we visited became the subject and object of their work. Theo created a three-dimensional

Figure 7.1 Documentation of Theo and Zoe walking and collaborating

church that looked charred on the outside (see Figure 7.1). He was struck by our visit to the Bethel Missionary Baptist Church, the spiritual home of Rev. C.K. Steele, and by the photograph we shared of Steele holding a burnt cross in the front yard of the church. Although Theo decided early on that he was interested in Bethel Baptist as the focus for his artmaking, he struggled to stay on task. Noticing Theo's waning interest, one of the teacher/researchers suggested returning to the church. In her field notes, she wrote, "that afternoon, I walked him to Bethel Baptist Church, where we were able to take a look inside the building and see an oil painting of C.K. Steele on the wall. Theo took pictures of the stained-glass windows and the pews and the pulpit. We continued to help him brainstorm the meanings behind the items in his project." Theo later explained the significance of the church and his glowing data in his exit interview:

> I'm making, like, a sculpture, I guess you could say, of a church, of the Bethel Baptist Church, and I'm putting bricks and stuff on it, and I'm gonna have a cross in front of the church. When Wilhelmina Jakes and Casey Patterson, they were, they refused to get out [of] their seat in the bus, and so that night the KKK, they got, they got a cross and they put it in front of their yard and burned it. And the next day, C.K. Steele went to go get it, and he put it in front of the church and showed everybody how the KKK treated them, treated the community … just for not getting out of their seat.

We asked him why he picked that moment and place as his glowing data. He quickly responded "Because it meant a lot, it meant a lot to us. It meant a lot because like, they were not treating us as fair as they were treating other people. They thought of us as just … objects." The Bethel Missionary Baptist Church was a site that gave Theo a sense of place. Tellingly, by the end of the week, he referred to the civil rights movement in Tallahassee as something he was personally implicated in: the actions are about an "us," naming a social space and collective spirit that included Theo.

Zoe also tuned in to the collective spirit of both our summer program and a social movement. She began her research with Patricia Stephens Due's case file, with the aid of an extensive collection of papers in the state archives.

Historical note

Patricia Stephens Due committed her life to the pursuit of civil rights, beginning at just 13 she refused to leave the White Only line at the Dairy Queen. Knowing the impact that young people can have on their world, she dedicated much of her time teaching other young people about the Black struggle for freedom. Due, along with Bethel Baptist's Reverend C.K. Steele and his son Henry Steele, among others, was a leading participant in the country's first jail in. She attended Florida A&M University (FAMU) in Tallahassee, beginning in the fall of 1957. In the summer of 1959, Due attended a workshop on non-violent civil disobedience hosted by CORE and after that she organized the lunch counter sit-in at Woolworth. She went on to marry John Due, a prominent civil rights attorney, and continued her long-standing commitment to the struggle for civil rights.

(Patricia Stephens Due, 2022)

Zoe commented that if Patricia Stephens Due were a musical instrument she would have been "a trumpet, because her actions were bold, loud, and confident" (see Figure 7.1). This confidence is something Zoe tapped into when working on her artistic research project, and ultimately when she chose to write a song honoring the spirit of the civil rights activists. Walking and seeing people, artifacts, and places in Tallahassee "through her own eyes" empowered Zoe to write a song focused on different activists (see Figure 7.1). She wanted to make a song about the movement as a whole. In her song, Break Free, the lyrics announced:

Verse 1

C.K. Steele boycotting the bus
He knew our race didn't define us
Racism was taking over
Gotta stand-up be strong be a soldier

Chorus

Its time to break free break free for you and me
time to break free cause that's the way that it should be

Part 1

We'd sit in jail just to prove a point
Than sit there doing nothing and just disappoint
We would rather walk in dignity than ride in humiliation
Standing for our entire nation

Chorus

It's time to break free break free for you and me
Time to break free cause that's the way that it should be

Verse 2

Black nurse Black doctors' takin care of their own
Healing the souls and fixing the bones
Preach peace and love
Black nurse Black doctors' takin care of their own
Healing the souls and fixing the bones
Preach peace and love
Even though it was tough

Chorus

It's time to break free, Break free for you and me
time to break free cause that's the way that it should be

Part 2

Know that in your heart you're right
Keep on fighting the good fight
We'd rather walk in dignity than ride in … Humiliation Standing for
our entire nation

Chorus

It's time to break free break free for you and me
Time to break free cause that's the way that it should be

Zoe was an energizing presence at camp, pulling in collaborators to help sing her chorus (see Figure 7.1). To record it, she asked everyone to join her on the last day in the practice rooms of the music building on campus. She distributed the lyrics of the refrain and patiently coached everyone to sing together: "I'd rather walk in dignity, than ride in humiliation." The recording of the voices of all the students singing together holds hope and communicates the power of a collective spirit. Zoe's song documented the energy of the movement, as it seemed to channel a collective call to action. The places we visited in our program held songs of protest and these songs, like Zoe's, brought together groups of people who forged a place of belonging, despite the landscape of hatred that surrounded them. While Zoe did not mention specific places in her song, her song did the work of creating a place where the teens came together to sing, and when singing, they could place themselves in relation to the legacy of those that came before them.

We believe it was this sense of belonging that brought Theo back to our program in 2019. A year older and, perhaps, a little more ready to engage in the project, Theo returned with a level of focus that he didn't have the prior summer. When we asked him why this project was important enough to come back and do again, he said "I think it's important because we need to learn about some history sometimes. Sometimes you need a lot more to understand and figure out what happened back then ... So you know how you got here today."

As the week started, he immediately teamed up with the other returning students and acted as a mentor of sorts, giving people an idea of what was coming up and how to best engage in each day. The first day we visited Bethel Baptist church, where he shared with others what he had learned about that location last year in his research and artmaking. He returned to campus to make a collage out of rubbings collected at that site, using rubbings of bricks and the church name. When asked about the visit to Bethel Baptist church and the collage of rubbings he made, he shared "how I made my rubbing ... That's when I first got the idea of what I was going to do." It was at the site of the focus of his first summer inquiry that he found his way to Patricia Stephens Due, the focus of his 2019 project. When we asked why he chose her, he shared that she went to FAMU and his parents and grandparents had both attended there, as well. For Theo, a connection to place, not people, was what led him to select Due's case file. Places, especially the archives, continue to emerge as significant for Theo's second summer with us, but instead of re-creating a place like he did in 2018, he used resources from place to inspire his final piece.

Historical note

During the summer programs we visited the State Archives of Florida and the Meek-Eaton Black Archives and Museum. The State Archives of Florida, located in downtown Tallahassee houses archival documents, including policy documents, correspondence written by government officials, newspapers, and donated collections, among other materials. The documents are sorted into carton boxes and stored in a climate controlled room the size of a warehouse, which presents an impressive physical display to students who can marvel at the sheer volume of the material. Notably, the archives contain the Patricia Stephens Due Papers collection, which total over 14 cubic feet and document Due's experiences as an activist. This collection was donated by Due's family and captures the work of CORE and SNCC, the correspondence Due and her sister had during their nationally renowned jail-in, and provides a full snapshot of the day-to-day activities that built the civil rights movement. The Meek-Eaton Black Archives and Museum is located on the campus of Florida A&M University, a short distance from the state archives. The majority of this archive consists of documents and records related to the history of Africans and African Americans. The archives has a highlighted focus on Black institutions and organizations, and also highlights the accomplishments of individuals of African descent in the Tallahassee area. The Meek-Eaton Black Archives and Museum hold a large number of books, journals, magazines, maps, photographs and newspapers. Like the state archives' collection of artifacts related to the civil rights movement, the vast majority of the Meek-Eaton archive has been donated by local individuals and organizations.

(FAMU. n.d.)

Theo reflected on the visits to the archives saying "they both showed a lot of history about Tallahassee [and] what has gone on in the city ... it impacted me because it showed me like how ... I guess kind of famous Patricia [Stephens Due} was ... she pretty famous, because like when we went to both the archives all the letters she got and she was often spoken about." Due's fame remained with Theo as he decided to create a vision of her as the statue of liberty, positioning her as a beacon of hope in her pursuit of civil rights (see Figure 7.1). In the last two days, Theo worked on his portrait, painting Due a copper-aged green tone "to represent her [as] the Statue of Liberty." He also added bright colors and glitter because he liked "how it made her around her look like she was very important."

His portrait stands out among the other completed artworks at the end of the week, a striking image of Due holding photocopies of the letters Theo found in the archives, correspondence which she sent and received during her time participating in the civil rights movement (see Figure 7.1). Across two summers, for Theo, place began as a literal way of representing his learning about the Bethel Baptist Church and its important role in the civil rights movement. Then, place evolved into a touchstone for connecting with history, as he engaged in the two visits to archives and returned to the church to collect rubbings. While his final project was a portrait of a person, he portrayed her as perhaps the most widely known landmark in our country, the Statue of Liberty. Looming large, her presence signifies the place of activists in history, and activism as a place of possibility. It was this fight for freedom and possibility, the pursuit of hope, that Theo sought to honor in his portrait of Patricia Stephens Due.

Resonance

Looking at Zoe and Theo's journey, we return to Theo's use of the collective word "us," and the following refrain from Zoe's song: "We'd rather walk in dignity than ride in humiliation. Standing for our entire nation." Both

Zoe and Theo were inspired by being in places, walking places, but most importantly, doing this work together. Visiting places in this program was, for Zoe and Theo, a way to join together in the present and the past, placing themselves within a collective history. Theo started with a site he visited and revisited and, in his second summer, was inspired by the archives. In both places, he carefully listened for the whispers of the past. Conversely, Zoe immersed herself in the social space of collective action, walking through her city alongside her friends, as she learned about activists that had walked before her. When talking about the history of the civil rights movement, both spoke from a plural first-person perspective, using the term us or we, situating themselves as within the movement's ongoing history. The places they visited introduced them to a movement, and grounded them in the memory of those who had sustained it. This tangible connection gave them an insight into personal stories and a sense of belonging with the community that built the movement.

Viola's topsy-turvy doll

Next, we will share the experiences and journey of Viola, an AP art student who attended a public high school in the city. Viola attended both summer programs and was a regular attendee to the monthly Saturday meetings that met during the school year, as an extension of that first summer experience. By the second year of the program, Viola had already developed a sense of the civil rights movement in Tallahassee, building on her understanding of the role of art in processing and honoring this movement.

Like the walking from the previous case, the Meek-Eaton Black Archives stood out in our closing interviews as an impactful moment in the week-long program. We visited this site only in 2019, the second summer of our program. On our first visit as teacher/researchers we toured the public-facing museum component of the archives with a docent and discussed with him the tour our students would take later in the summer. The museum is large, and its rooms are each organized around a theme or era. Upstairs, the docent led us first through a room honoring the role of faith and religion within Black communities. In this space, several stained-glass windows are preserved from the Bethel Baptist Church, dating from when Rev. C. K. Steele was pastor, along with the bullet holes left in them after a racist attack. These windows are not, necessarily, the focus of this room, but one component of the materials holding history in this space. On display are the everyday objects that bear witness to events that continue to shape our present. Across the hallway, the docent paused his tour, explaining that the museum does not always include the next room on educational tours due to the racist content it holds. Inside is a collection of artifacts including, for example, postcards and souvenirs with Alligator

Bait imagery, Ku Klux Klan attire and propaganda, and a topsy-turvy doll. After viewing this space, we discussed with the docent whether or not to include this room on the tour with the students. We recalled our experience from the prior summer when we viewed a documentary about the reopening of the investigation into Emmett Till's murder. We recalled how the students talked to each other, asked questions, shared their feelings of anger, shock, and grief, and engaged in dialogue. We trusted them to be able to view this space and ultimately decided to include it in our visit.

In conversation with Viola, this visit to the museum was mentioned as the highlight of her week. During her tour of the museum, she was impacted by the weight of history contained within the objects there, drawn to the stories they tell, and to the strong sense of witness they offer. Viola reflected, "I really enjoyed the FAMU Black Archives. I just like that there's so much in Tallahassee that's not talked about and there's a bunch of history here, and I really enjoyed going and seeing actual artifacts from that time period and how we got to learn about it." The visit to the museum, and the material objects encountered there, revealed a depth to the city she lives in and the culture she belongs to. Her experience in the museum illustrated how material objects can provide a sense of place, and how a museum allows students to place themselves in history. Thinking about the objects she encountered, Viola commented,

for me it was … there's two things, it was the room with the slave shackles, and the feeding trough whatever it was called and all that… That was, like, really hard for me to look at because I was like, wow this actually, like *really*, happened. And the room with the KKK and stuff … that room was, was so stereotypical of what they think we looked like and that made me say, like, oh this really happened, this really is a thing.

Of course, Viola was not suggesting that the information in the museum was new to her, she was aware of the history of racism during Jim Crow and the era of slavery in the United States. Instead, Viola was processing how the museum objects allowed her to engage with this history differently. In the museum, the past appeared closer, and more real. We were moved watching Viola grapple with the complex history the museum contains. In response to the museum visit, Viola wrote in her field guide:

I felt regret, anger, and many other emotions, by seeing how cruel people like me we [sic] treated back in those times. I am baffled that people can be so cruel to one another just because of skin color … I had never fully grasped the idea of people who looked like me being able to have that much power and authority to bring about change.

Her strong, emotional response to the objects of violence did not deter Viola from seeing a narrative of strength and accomplishment. Interestingly, the artmaking Viola engaged with seemed to elaborate on this complex narrative. Viola was inspired by an object she came across in the museum, a topsy-turvy doll (see Figure 7.2). Her project reinterpreted this

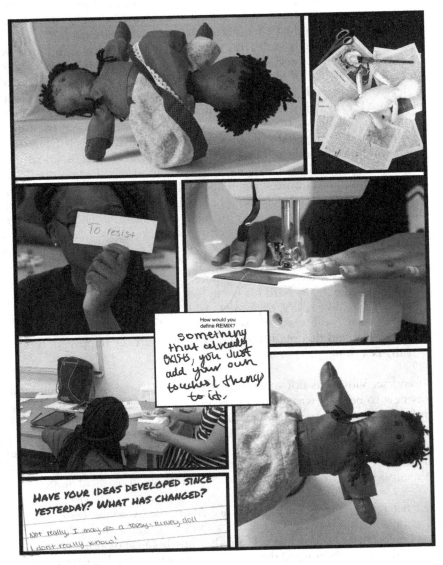

Figure 7.2 Documentation of Viola's topsy-turvy doll

object for her final piece in 2019. However, rather than contain one White and one Black figure as was typical of such dolls, in her doll both figures were Black (see Figure 7.2).

Historical note

The topsy-turvy doll is two-headed and two-bodied—one Black body and one White, conjoined at the lower waist where the hips and legs would ordinarily be. The lining of one's dress is the outside of the other's, so that the skirt flips over to conceal one body when the other is upright. ... The topsy-turvy doll, as it's known, most likely originated in American plantation nurseries of the early 19th century. By the mid-20th century, they'd grown so popular that they were mass-manufactured and widely available in department stores across the country, but today, they're found mostly in museums, private collections, and contemporary art ... It's unclear whether topsy-turvy dolls were first created to reinforce racial and sexual power dynamics or if they were something more subversive. Either way, the dolls have, since the beginning, been reinterpreted and appropriated to suit the use of their makers, the children who played with them, and the people who felt they were worth preserving—their purpose was always context-dependent, a moving mirror of racial womanhood.

(Jarboe, 2015, n.p.)

Tracing the evolution of her project, we note how Viola responded to the materials in the museum through a careful material practice of her own. In response to a prompt in her field guide, asking what action the museum visit inspired, she wrote, "I am inspired to love myself and those who look like me ..." Later, in a discussion about her piece, Viola confronted both her anger and her wish to focus on a more positive narrative. She commented,

With my doll, I think [the theme] is more of, like, equality—not for, like, everyone but for women because it's obviously a girl—also, I think, beauty standards. Because, the one we saw in the Black archives, it's like a White and a Black one and basically telling kids that although we're born this, you can become this. So, mine is basically just to show that if you're dark, it's fine, you're still beautiful. And you don't have to be like this, you don't have to be the European standard of beauty, you can be your own standard of beauty, it's OK.

For Viola, the topsy-turvy doll represented an invitation to replace harmful imagery with a more positive message. She was thoughtful about this in her making,

> I think the hardest part of [my project] was trying to get the message across without having it being seen as negative … So like for the doll, I originally wanted them to be Black and White but then I'm like wait, people are going to read that wrong! So, let's just make it both Black so I get the point across and not have to have people question why.

Viola's project is a thoughtful contribution to a specific genre of objects. Her initial interest in the object came from her critique of it: she understood the object juxtaposes Black and White beauty standards, imposing a binary that is meant to elevate Whiteness. Her instinct to call out this object is centered on the call to action she has charted for herself, one that is invested in "loving herself and those who look like her." In reconfiguring the doll, Viola demonstrated her understanding that merely pointing to a problematic object is not enough, instead, she knew it had to be altered. By making a doll of two Black girls, the project rejected the binary that compares Black to White and validated, as Viola mentioned, that beauty does not have to be measured within the frame of Whiteness (see Figure 7.2).

Here we return to Viola's call to action, providing her full written reflection: "I am inspired to love myself and those who look like me. I want to share their stories so people know reality vs. what false news is put out." Viola was responding to the false representation of Black people found in the collection of racist memorabilia she saw on display in the museum. Recall her reaction: "I am baffled that people can be so cruel to one another just because of skin color." The false perception of Blackness that permeates racist imagery (and racist thought) is what Viola was working to critique in her project. Important to our larger discussion, this project revealed the role an object may have in working against the cry of "fake news" that we so often must confront today. Viola's interest in the doll was a response to her understanding that objects make history real—they are evidence that something, as Viola noted, "really happened." In today's environment where discussions of systemic racism are politicized and disavowed, Viola's work made a powerful case for the relevancy of historical objects, illustrating how artifacts, and specifically archives, hold pieces of evidence that bear witness to and preserve a cultural moment from the past, which refuses to be erased or forgotten in the present and future.

Resonance

Viola's artmaking responded to a call to action she wrote for herself, as she set out to respond to the history of racism by offering an alternative representation of Black girlhood as worthy and valuable. We see the importance of a site visit to the museum as central to her project. The Meek-Eaton Black Archives and Museum allowed Viola to confront a racist past that may not get full representation or recognition in other spaces, such as at school. While there was difficulty felt when confronting this racism, the museum was also a site of pride. As an artist, Viola tuned in to the power of being in a place that is dedicated to collecting, displaying, and learning from material objects. Through her appropriation of one of these objects, she worked to turn a harmful stereotype into an affirmation of worth. The museum and its objects thus represent a powerful place-based learning opportunity for Viola to engage in inquiry, critical reflection, and participation as she responded to the multiple narratives she encountered there. Finding herself reflected in the history of this place was an invitation for her to become part of it.

Conclusion

As we slowly took in the city together, talking, laughing, and walking, the memory of the past collided with the present. Visiting sites, overlapping them with historical photographs, the teens made connections with history. Conversing and sharing this with friends, they were no longer looking at the history you learn about in school, but producing their own histories-in-the-making. The act of walking through Tallahassee and visiting the archives to see objects from the past, blurred the lines between past and present, and sparked imagination and speculation. By engaging on the ground level and changing their perspective, the teens were able to put themselves inside historical moments. Visiting places pushed them to ask questions about who else had stood in this spot or held this object. They considered what had taken place here, and what these experiences were like. As the students contemplated this, withering in a heat that surely bore down on activists decades earlier, we imagine they found themselves recognizing the everydayness of history. A church, a doll, a letter, the fact that the everyday sites and the objects belonging to them are not particularly unique is telling. Teens were perhaps confronted with the fact that history happened in everyday places, and that history was made by people just like them. We saw students come into the realization that our moment is history in the making, that history was once a day just like today, holding potential for a different future.

Physical places and objects carry the past into present environments, in ways that allow students to touch, and possibly manipulate, history. Contemporary art practice also offers us strategies for being in the world, differently. Site-specific work, installations, public interventions, or creative placemaking projects signal the ways in which art can weave itself into the fabric of our environments, honoring and also creating community. Working from a critical perspective, these interventions can contribute to a project of reinhabitation and decolonization (Gruenewald, 2003). In Theo's and Zoe's case study, we look at how students tuned in to the practice of reinhabitation and decolonization within the civil rights movement, taking inspiration from the way activists occupied spaces, created community, and pushed ahead with a new vision of what it meant to live well. This learning took place for them as a result of an invitation to engage with the materiality of urban blocks, the summer heat, photographs, archives, and historic sites. Using sites and artifacts offered an embodied way for students to engage with history, making it tangible and alive. Taking our city as a starting point shone light on how people take their own place in history, connecting students to a sense of community and purpose. Standing in the present, rooted in the past, the students found that the city offered both a place and a social space of transformational learning.

Furthermore, our students demonstrated that artwork has a specific relation to place and can make its own contribution. Monuments, artworks, artifacts, and museums typically form part of the art curriculum, suggesting the role art can play in the historical narratives of communities. Freire (1998) suggested that learning is connected to place. He framed literacy as a project of "reading the world." For Freire, reading the world is a literacy practice that both mirrors and extends beyond an individual's ability to read the word; he insisted that context, like text, must be studied, comprehended, interpreted, and analyzed. Importantly, reading the world is a framework that values the situationality and cultural knowledge of individual students. This critical framework is a foundation for the place-centered learning adapted by our summer art intensive program.

Places, as a site for student-led research, include the local culture as well as the natural environment as a starting point (Smith, 2002). It is possible to see a connection emerge that links this approach with a notion of citizenship, one where students' connection and contribution to their community is central. These kinds of inquiries begin in local communities and should be experiential, engaged, and transformative:

> Emphasizing hands-on, real-world learning experiences this approach to education increases academic achievement, helps students develop stronger ties to their community, enhances students' appreciation for

the natural world, and creates a heightened commitment to serving as active, contributing citizens.

(Sobel, 2004, p. 7)

When places are central to learning experiences, we found that young people spoke about their own relationship with the city differently. We recall Theo and Zoe's closing interviews where they shared that they now noticed places in Tallahassee differently. Places are not only a starting point for studying what is local, place-based learning offers a method for integrating students into their community. This approach engages students in curriculum that is directly relevant to them, incorporates hands-on experiential learning strategies, and aims to turn students into a resource for their community. When students engage and take ownership of their communities the notion of living well often emerges:

> [L]earning that is rooted in what is local—the unique history, environment, culture, economy, literature, and art of a particular place. The community provides the context for learning, student work focuses on community needs and interests, and community members serve as resources and partners in teaching and learning. Place-based educators have discovered that this local focus has the power to engage students academically ... while promoting genuine citizenship and preparing people to respect and live well in any community they choose.

(Rural School and Community Trust, 2003;
see Gruenewald, 2005)

The implication in living well is that students should have the opportunity to not only know, but become part of community life. In this way, the idea of living well requires a critical approach to learning about community (Gruenewald, 2003). By asking students to live well, place-based approaches to doing history and making art ask students to be part of building places into the kinds of communities that support them.

When we ask students to study places, we are interested in the living histories these places hold on to; the monuments, historic sites, and museums are significant for the stories they contain. When we ask students to stand in history, the reflection we hope it leads to is how they, too, may take their own place in this narrative. Through this work, we approach civic education as a practice of building a social space, where students' sphere of action is rooted in physical ties to local politics, but also encompasses a community made up of personal relationships. As we reflect on the impact that thinking and making with places had on the civic capacities of our youth participants, we acknowledge the slippery nature of the notion of place. Both physical and social, historical and unfolding, place was a process; and its constructed nature became an invitation for action.

References

FAMU (n.d.). *The Black Archives Collection.* https://www.famu.edu/academics/libraries/mark-eaton-black-archives-research-center-and-museum/meba-collections.php

Freire, P. (1998). Reprint: Cultural action and conscientization. *Harvard Educational Review*, 68(4), 499. https://doi.org/10.17763/haer.68.4.656ku47213445042

Gruenewald, D. A. (2003). The best of both worlds: A critical pedagogy of place. *Educational Researcher*, 32(4), 3–12. https://doi.org/10.3102/0013189x032004003

Gruenewald, D. A. (2005). Accountability and collaboration: Institutional barriers and strategic pathways for place-based education. Ethics, Place and Environment, 8(3), 261–283. https://doi.org/10.1080/13668790500348208

Jarboe, J. K. (2015) The racial symbolism of the topsy-turvy Doll. *The Atlantic.* https://www.theatlantic.com/technology/archive/2015/11/the-racial-symbolism-of-the-topsy-turvy-doll/416985/

Patricia Stephens Due. (2022). Biography. The history makers: The digital repository for the Black experience. https://www.thehistorymakers.org/biography/patricia-stephens-due-41

Smith, G. A. (2002). Place-based education: Learning to be where we are. *Phi Delta Kappa*, 83(8), 584–594. https://doi.org/10.1177/003172170208300806

Sobel, D. (2004). *Place-based education: Connecting classrooms and community.* Orion Society Press.

8 Researching Events

Chapters 6 and 7 discussed people and places as significant starting and ending points for students to engage in arts-based research and develop civic dispositions and skills. Now we shift to considering what happens when you view people and places as the components making up historical events. Events, unlike people and places, are not tangible. You cannot interview or visit a historical event; instead, they remain an abstraction of a moment once occupied by people and places from the past. While people and places are the ephemera of events, they also contribute to the trickiness of remembering and researching them. Events are made up of varied and often vastly different memories; to further complicate the matter, events are often recalled from a particular historical perspective or vantage point. This complication is what makes collective memory so important to the work in this book. Collective memory challenges history, it is "not substituting history for memory, but of continuously reworking the relation between history and collective memory" (Ricoeur, 2004, p. 388). In the Foot Soldier program, we approach historical events as a project of collective memory, asking students to engage them in an attempt to carry events from the past into present-day considerations. We used the concept of events to consider what impact history had, and still has, on us today. Following Vosloo (2012), we believed, "history has to bridge the distance, difference and dislocation between present and past, the past and the present are already more intimately connected in the case of memory, with the agency of the individual playing a central role" (p. 218).

By calling upon a series of significant events and giving students access to the stories of people and places, we asked students to rework the version of history they were taught by bringing historical events into their own sphere of understanding. As students walked the streets of our city and listened to stories, they engaged with the memories of historical moments held within familiar signposts of their city and voices from the community. Immersed in history as a project of memory, students imagined how history continues to work on us, and began to see how historical events have brought them, and the city, to the place they are today.

DOI: 10.4324/9781003199106-11

In this chapter, we look at illustrative cases where teens engaged in the work of remembering historical events. We see this process as deeply connected to the notion of *doing history* that we introduced in Chapter 4. Here we will look at how students were able to develop, after a close consideration of how historical events are impacted by individual actions or collective decisions, sophisticated interpretations of contemporary events based on their engagement with collective memory.

Ruby's then and now

In this illustrative case, we follow Ruby's journey through the program, in the second summer, to contemplate how students can be drawn into learning about history. This work unfolds by interrogating and participating in the collective memory work that holds histories together. Ruby was a sophomore student enrolled in a large, urban high school located in the center of town. During the program, Ruby, who is biracial, reflected on her personal heritage as she wondered how the history of the civil rights movement related to her. Ruby was raised by all White family members, who have deep roots in a rural town just outside of Tallahassee. Her father and his family are Black, first generation Africans, who did not have enslaved ancestors. Ruby commented during the program that her history as a Black person was not the same as that of many Black Americans, although she felt that she was often perceived as sharing this history. The question of how this history related to her was one that felt complex and not fully resolved; Ruby was interested in it but did not want to claim a historical legacy that was not her own. Mid-way through the program, Ruby reflected that perhaps her personal connection to the topic stemmed mostly from the fact that the more she learned about the civil rights movement, the more passionate she became. At the end of the program, she reflected:

> It was really strong for me to actually see [in the Black Archives] like what happened in my history, or compared to what might have happened in another African American's history, does that make sense? So, and I don't really, I don't talk to my dad very much, but it's a really good way to look at things and be able to access your own history, even if normally, you don't have access to your history.

At the start of the week, Ruby chose a case file on LeRoy Collins, a White man who served as governor of Florida from 1955 to 1961. Collins is remembered for changing his approach to integration measures once in office, coming to support national desegregation efforts, despite originally campaigning against the issue. We suspect Ruby chose this case file because she was familiar with the governor; in her early notes about what she knew about the civil rights movement, she mentioned desegregation in Florida and Tallahassee's role in it. Between these notes and her research into Collins, Ruby seemed focused on the event of desegregation, which she also referenced in her field guide at the beginning of the week. For example, describing a collage that features the word free she made on the second day (see Figure 8.1), she wrote, "I'm talking about the freedom served by making segregation illegal."

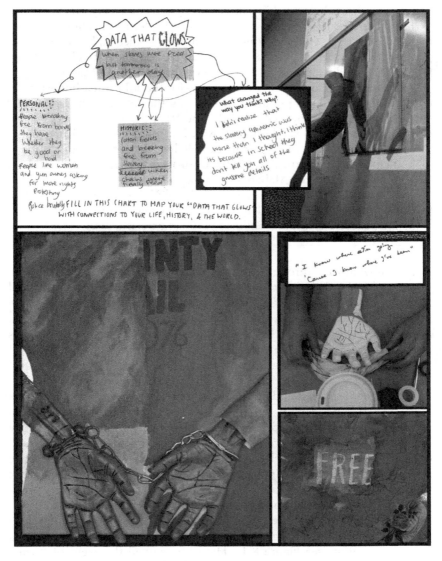

Figure 8.1 Documentation of Ruby's then and now

Historical note

After serving in the state senate from 1940 to 1953, Thomas LeRoy Collins became Governor of Florida during a special election in 1954. In 1956, Collins was reelected to the governorship. During his initial gubernatorial campaign, Collins was in favor of segregation, however his beliefs on this matter changed dramatically once in office. After the 1954 Brown vs. the Board of Education ruling by the Supreme Court, Collins adopted a pragmatic stance and took measures to ensure that Florida did not oppose the federal ruling. His advocacy and support for segregation grew over time. After leaving office in 1961, Collins went on to work for the Johnson administration, when he was appointed to serve as the first Director of the Community Relations Service under the 1964 Civil Rights Act. This position led him to work directly with Dr. Martin Luther King, Jr., through the Southern Christian Leadership Conference, and state and city agencies in the mid-1960s. Collins coordinated closely with King and the state of Alabama to mitigate the risk of police brutality during the march on Selma. A photo of Collins and King taken during this march was used against Collins when he ran for the U.S. Senate, effectively ending Collins's political career.

As Ruby moved through the program, the historical narratives she referenced expanded. After visiting the Meek-Eaton Black Archives and Museum on the third day, Ruby's focus on desegregation shifted. At the museum, she was impacted by the brutality of slavery evidenced there. She wrote in her field guide, "I didn't realize the slavery epidemic was worse than I thought, I think it's because at school they don't tell you all the gruesome details." Reflecting on how her feelings changed as a result of this visit, she added, "at first I felt grateful that we overcame slavery, but then I felt ashamed and angry and sad about how African Americans were treated." We cannot tell from her notes if the treatment she was referring to was a reference to slavery, or a reference to contemporary discrimination, although we know the Meek-Eaton Black Archives held evidence of both. Ultimately, we find the ambiguity of her notes to be representative of Ruby's thinking, as she spent the second part of the week thinking about how the legacy of slavery is present in contemporary problems, specifically in relation to the mass incarceration of Black men.

Once our program shifted to individual project planning and development, Ruby filled out a page in her field guide that prompted her to discuss her main interest (see Figure 8.1). Here, she named the event of "when slaves were freed." The prompt asked Ruby to thread the past and present together. Here, the past emerged through a visual metaphor: "cotton fields and breaking free from slavery/when chains were finally freed." For the present, her personal connection to this topic introduced contemporary references, "people breaking free from bonds they have whether they be good or bad/people like women and gun owners asking for more rights/protesting/police brutality."

After introducing a unit on creative remixing at the end of the third day, Ruby was once again prompted to reflect on her creative project in relation to the information she had learned so far. In her notes she developed her thinking; in response to the prompt, *list some of your ideas*, she wrote, "hand with broken chain with background sunset, with cotton plants plantation/plaster." In a group discussion, she described her vision of making hands bound by a chain, specifying that one hand would have a shackle and the other a handcuff (see Figure 8.1). The juxtaposition between enslavement and incarceration moved her work forward. When production began, she worked with model magic to make her sculpture (see Figure 8.1). At the end of day four, in a peer critique circle, Ruby got help from peers; together they discussed where her sculpture could be mounted, and another student–Dwayne–suggested painting a back as a background to the sculpture. He added, half the back could be a jumpsuit and the other half painted to represent an enslaved person. Ruby was excited about this suggestion. Suddenly, her piece was taking shape. She worked with the instructors to find a source image for the painting, combining two images from the internet, and tracing the image onto a canvas (see Figure 8.1). The impending deadline on the last day of the program pushed Ruby, and the other students, to wrap up their work. On this day, she hastily painted the background in acrylic, finishing the piece by mounting her sculpture over it.

Reflecting on Ruby's process, we note how she worked backward and forward in time, moving from an understanding of a historical event as something that happened, to an understanding of history as continuing in the present. In her exit interview, she spoke carefully about this ongoing sense of historic events:

> I guess I'm trying to make the theme of bondage in the past still being representative of the future. Even though things have happened that may have freed some bondages, for some people, but even in the past, like I said before, things are reoccurring. Even though we don't want to repeat history, it is still happening.

By the end of the week, Ruby transitioned from focusing on the past as a record of history, to understanding how historical events take place over

time, interacting and influencing our present and future. In her artist statement, she claimed, "[My project] looks like a symbol of slavery and police
brutality … I am inspired by the fact that the past repeats itself."

Resonance

Ruby could not separate her learning of history from her understanding
of collective memory. While Ruby moved through her inquiry, she was reflecting on the nature of history and its connection to personal experience.
In response to an interview question asking what she had learned about
Tallahassee, she shared the following:

> I learned a lot from my grandparents who are Caucasian, so I learned
> a lot of, I guess, their side of the story when it comes to the civil
> rights movement. My grandpa is from here and my grandma is
> from Havana [a rural town near Tallahassee]. And so they told me
> a lot about how—I guess, there was like a gray area of people who
> weren't fighting against segregation, and people who were fighting
> for it. And, so, they [her grandparents] were just kind of in the gray
> area like that, they weren't discriminating or anything like that. So I
> heard a lot from how they were, when they were kids. But learning
> about Tallahassee and about the activists we got to meet was, like, an
> eye opener for actually getting another side of the story. So, I got to
> learn a lot about how it was for other people, so that was really cool.

In this reflection, we hear an understanding of how a historical event, like
desegregation, holds multiple perspectives. Ruby appears curious about
the role of evolving historical narratives in expanding her understanding
of history as ongoing. In this process, Ruby seemed aware of how race
impacts frameworks for interpreting history; White people are allowed a
gray area, while Black people are fighting for their lives.

This process of perspective taking was an invitation for Ruby to move
from relating to history as something from the past, to thinking about
the ongoing work of *doing* history. This learning occurs in the process of
artmaking. Here, the remix prompt was pivotal, as this artistic practice
became a metaphor for bringing history into the present. As a result,
Ruby moved from writing about emancipation as a discrete event—when
slaves broke free—to reflecting on the systemic nature of Black confine-
ment in the United States as it relates to the legacy of slavery. By engaging creatively with history, Ruby demonstrated how working with the
past provided fodder for discussing contemporary issues. In this way,
remixing not only engaged students with contemporary art practices, it
also offered a lesson about the larger project of doing history and holding

on to multiple narratives and perspectives. Through her process, Ruby began to frame history as an event unfolding in the present. In her exit interview, she reflected: "there's stages and stages. A lot of people will fight for [their rights] and then it's, somehow, a result. And then there's more people fighting for something else. So, I do feel, like, it's important for people to stand up and do what's important to them, because then it encourages other people." Ultimately, she learned that doing history can be an invitation to carry on its legacy. By focusing on the nature of events, history is framed as a term that is as much related to the future, as it is to the past.

Hannah's forgotten figures

Hannah, a White, 13-year-old, self-reported introvert, was a rising 8th grader at a local K-12 charter school. Prior to the Foot Soldier program, Hannah had participated in other summer experiences we offered at Florida State University, including attending two consecutive years of our summer camp. Hannah was familiar with some of the research team and had a clear drawing style she had developed across the summer camps she attended. Hannah described herself as being "in the shadow" and not "being in the spotlight a lot," a theme that emerged over the week as central to how she built an understanding of events through collective memory.

On our first day, Hannah selected a case study file on Rev. C. K. Steele. Steele, unlike many of the foot soldiers featured in the field guides, was a central, visible, vocal figure in the official history about the civil rights movement in Tallahassee. As such, there was a wealth of information about him and his advocacy work in almost all the sites we visited throughout the week.

Historical note

Rev. C.K. Steele was the pastor of Bethel Baptist Church from 1952-1980 and a central figure of the civil rights movement locally and nationally. Not long after Rosa Parks was arrested and Martin Luther King, Jr. organized the bus boycotts in Alabama, two Florida A&M (FAMU) students were arrested in Tallahassee for sitting in the White-only section of the city bus. Steele was the local representative of the National Association for the Advancement of Colored People (NAACP) at the time, and he worked closely with FAMU students to organize and lead a bus boycott that stretched over 8 months. As a result of his organizing, the Cities Transit Company in Tallahassee was obliged to hire Black drivers, remove seating ordinances, and

expand routes. Today, StarMetro, Tallahassee's bus system, operates out of a central hub named after C. K. Steele. In addition to his
work on the bus boycott, C. K. Steele worked closely with Martin
Luther King, Jr., helping found the Southern Christian Leadership
Conference (SCLC). He also pursued lawsuits that forced desegregation of local schools, fought against unjust business practices,
and served as a state level president for the NAACP. Steele was a
shining light in the civil rights movement, and his legacy lives on
in Tallahassee through murals, and a major roadway and the bus
station named in his honor.

(The Martin Luther King, Jr. Research and
Education Institute, n.d.)

After choosing his case file, Hannah delved deeper into C. K. Steele's
legacy during an early visit to the state archives. In her closing interview
she said "When I was there and just kind of looking around, I was trying
to figure out why there were folders dedicated to just C. K. Steele and I saw
his name mentioned a bunch of times. I found out that he was in almost
every single flyer … It was crazy." She goes on later to say,

ever since I learned about him, I saw a road that said Memorial to C.
K. Steele. I've been seeing statues of him, and signs about him, and I
never saw that because I didn't even know who he was. Apparently
he was big in Tallahassee for helping us in the civil rights movement
and they don't teach about him at school whatsoever and that's kind
of like… what!?

This simple act of noticing something that had gone unnoticed began Hannah's investigation into C. K. Steele's legacy in Tallahassee. After we visited the bus plaza and rode the city bus, she reflected in her field guide
that she was surprised that his statue was not more centrally located. She
continued to research C. K. Steele, interested in his friendship with Martin
Luther King, Jr., his influence in the civil rights movement, and his exclu-
sion from the local K-12 curriculum. As the week progressed, her interest
shifted from C. K. Steele to include other key figures in the movement;
more specifically, she started to think about how the central figures of the
civil rights movement cast a shadow over all those supporting them (see
Figure 8.2). We see this thinking in her finished piece. On the far left you
see an eye, representing "everyone," shining a light on a group of people.
C. K. Steele is represented in the front, but behind him is a large group of
people, progressively obscured as Steele's shadow casts them into darkness
(see Figure 8.2).

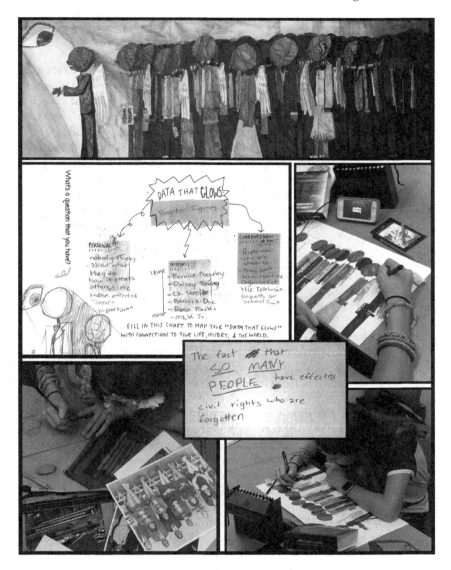

Figure 8.2 Documentation of Hannah's forgotten figures

Throughout the week Hannah struggled with how to recognize Steele without forgetting everyone else she was learning about. Mid-way through the
week, a group of women came to speak with us about their role in the first
Woolworth's lunch counter sit-in in Tallahassee. Because no arrests were made
during this protest, there is very little, if any, documentation of the event.

Historical note

Gloria Anderson and Bernice Presley came to the classroom to speak to the students on the third day of the program. The visit started with introductions, where each student introduced themselves and shared which case file they were researching. As they each took the time to introduce themselves and their case study, the women nodded and smiled as they recognized the names of the people that participated in the movement. During their visit they recounted the experience of growing up in Leon County during the height of the civil rights movement. Their visit spanned from a recounting of their experience in segregated schools, all the way through to their participation in the first Woolworth sit-in. This is Bernice Presley's account, transcribed from her talk with the students:

> There were seven of us and we had our training and went down to Woolworth's. I don't know what's in that spot right now, but we went down to Woolworth's. And we were told to go in… When we're there and we purchase something, and after that—See, I remember it as if it was yesterday cause it was such a part of me, yes—So, we were told to go to the counter and we skipped every other seat—you can't sit in consecutive seats. There were seven of us, so we sat down. As soon as we sat down, those waiters didn't look at us, they went to the back. They didn't even ask you, "would you like to have something?" So, we were supposed to sit there for 15 minutes. Reverend C. K. Steele was at the end of the counter, he had his newspaper, reading it. And then, after 15 minutes, he gave us a nod. And then we turned around. Everyone in the world was in Woolworth's, everybody in the world. I don't know how those people came in so quickly. And we had to go in a line, through all of that crowd. Now, we were told, you might get shot, you might get stabbed—We were prepared for all of that.
>
> So, when I sat at that counter with my back turned, don't think I wasn't afraid. I was afraid. But I'm saying, someone has to do it. I sat there and I prayed. So, we went through that crowd and we got in our vehicle and we came back to FAMU campus. And I think about two or three weeks later, the next group went down. And guess what? They were ready for them, policemen were waiting. But they were not ready for us, we shocked them. We shocked them but we were not arrested. So, the second group

> went down, and they were waiting for them; they spit on them, they called them names. So, they were finally arrested, they had to stay in jail overnight—that second group of students. Now those are the ones—Barbara Broxton, that you're talking about, John [Broxton], my friend. They stayed in jail overnight. And we stayed there—we did not sleep at night because we were waiting for them to come home. But seven of us don't have any history because they did not record us.

Hannah was inspired by their visit, she remarked in her closing interview, "it was kind of surprising to me, finding out a bunch of other people who were very very important ... One of them did the first sit-in and was just completely ignored. Nobody knew anything about her. So this is what I was trying to do with that [the artwork]. There are so many people who were part of this, who are trying to collect in the shadows [referencing the right side of her artwork]." As we talked to Hannah about her work it became clear that while the memory of these forgotten women from the civil rights movement was not her memory, their story resonated with her.

Later in the week, the field guides prompted students to record their glowing data (MacLure, 2010), or the information that stood out to them the most after the three days of research. In her field guide, Hannah wrote that what glowed for her was: "the fact that <u>SO MANY PEOPLE</u> have affected [sic] civil rights who are forgotten" (see Figure 8.2). Throughout the week she worked on a piece that remembered the forgotten faces and figures that stood behind C. K. Steele. She described the work saying, "there's always one big person, but there's also tons and tons of people who support them and help them get there, who have their own stories that may be interesting and important, but ignored."

Resonance

As we reflected on Hannah's work, we recalled her early reference to shadows, where she described herself as being in the shadows. The metaphor of the shadow becomes a significant idea for both Hannah and for the broader goals of this approach to education. We found resonance in the ability for Hannah to find an empathetic connection to someone who was so different from her, both culturally and generationally. We know this empathetic understanding is critical to being able to be civically engaged, "that social empathy and civic engagement work together in a dynamic process, each encouraging the development of the other" (Hylton, 2018, p. 93). Hannah's project began with a desire to learn more about one man who contributed significantly to the civil rights movement in Tallahassee, and ended with an acknowledgment that social movements and historical events are not attributed to just one person, but rather they stem from a myriad of stories and faces that are never heard or seen. These stories resonated with how Hannah saw herself, and revealed people who live in the shadows of the great figures that history remembers. In her work throughout the week, Hannah engaged in a deep and meaningful remembering of all of those who stood in the shadows. Hannah also created personal connections to a movement and moment in time that at one point felt unrelated and disconnected. This is the work of collective memory, finding ways to rework historical events and narratives to make them meaningful, personally and in the present. Before this week, Hannah said she had learned about the civil rights movement but not the movement in Florida specifically. She said, "cuz usually at school they explain like Americans are this great ... but they ignore all the little, nasty details." This excerpt from our interviews hints at the deeply complex relationship between collective memory and social empathy. While Hannah's day-to-day experience as a White teenager in Tallahassee were far removed from the experiences of the participants in the civil rights movement, her project highlighted how her empathetic connection with the people in the shadows of the movement pushed her to rewrite from within a collective memory of the movement, expanding that memory into the present, to include her own position and obligation to do better than those that came before her. In her final reflection we asked Hannah to share the salient take-aways she had from the week and she said,

> That everyone has a story and everyone has a moral to their own life .... It was really interesting to find that there were people that were forgotten, you don't think about, that you can hide so many messages in the little things that you do ... We can't brush it aside, we have to remember it so that we can at least honor these people who have put in all this effort and might have even died for this. ... Because, it's important to know our history, of course. It's important to know how we got to where we are so that you can have a better understanding.

Conclusion

For this project, the overarching event we studied was the civil rights movement, which is made up of hundreds of smaller events, each one representing a piece of the larger historical moment. In schools, the curriculum on the civil rights movement features a predictable host of people and places, i.e. Martin Luther King, Jr., Rosa Parks, Emmett Till, the Selma

Bridge, the Washington Mall, bus stations, and lunch counters. These figures and locations make up the nation's "master narrative" (Aldridge, 2006, p. 662) of the event of the civil rights movement, where the collective memory of this era is abstracted into a series of repeated actions–bus boycotts, sit-ins, marches, arrests, speeches–punctuated by a famous face or piece of landmark legislation. The students confirmed this, time and again, as they shared how surprised they were to learn about the events of the civil rights movement taking place in Tallahassee. One result of the master narrative obscuring the rich texture of historical events is that, for young people, history can feel like a memory belonging to someone else; it feels, as one student put it, "like make believe." (See Chapter 9 for a full discussion of students' sense of history.)

History, when taught as a series of isolated events, "allows the chaos of the past and the present to be reordered into stable binaries of authentic/simulated, heroes/villains and victims/oppressors. To be placed on either side of the slash can have serious political and material ramifications" (Hodgins, 2004, p. 100). In an effort to work against the dichotomy of us/them, we asked the teens in our project to look at the version of historical events they learned in schools and hold that alongside the collective memories offered by the people and places they were learning about. This alongsideness allowed them to exist in relation to history, to understand history as unfolding, continuously around them. As a pedagogical project, collective memory work counteracts the potential, long-standing ramifications master narratives may have on the ways that young people see themselves in relation to their communities.

> [D]ire predictions are sounded about cultural consequences of this collective loss of memory. Reasoning that memory is at the core of personal and collective identity, the prophets of amnesia warn us that if we do not somehow reconnect with some sort of authentic past, we are doomed to a life of alienation, anomie, loss of meaning and a feverish vacillation between fundamentalism and nihilistic hedonism.
>
> (Hodgins, 2004, p. 100)

To confront the alienation master narratives produce, collective memory work stands out as an approach to be used in the classroom. Wilson (2021) discussed this work, looking carefully at how social movements can serve as curriculum. He posited that "curricularizing social movements, transform[s] them into teaching and learning opportunities, creates connections for people to become readers and writers of their worlds, using memories of the past as conduits to reconstruct their futures" (Wilson, 2021, p. 34).

Ruby and Hannah showed us that their study of the civil rights movement was a study in surprising stories, in conflicting narratives, and in forging a connection between the personal and political, the past and the present. Taking up inquiry into a local issue, we saw that the more they learned, the more connected they felt to their community. This sense of connection to their community fostered a form of social empathy that can ultimately impact the trajectory of the present, binding students to an unfolding history dedicated to developing a more just future. This, then, is the power of civic engagement as it relates to historical events. By adopting an understanding that history is not of the past, but instead a product of ongoing collective memory, emerging through processes of sharing and storying, students and teachers can see a role for themselves in capturing and continuing this unfolding moment.

References

Aldridge, D. (2006). The limits of master narratives in history textbooks: An analysis of representations of Martin Luther King, Jr. *Teachers College Record, 108*(4), 662–686. https://doi.org/10.1111/j.1467-9620.2006.00664.x

Hodgins, P. (2004). Our haunted present: Cultural memory in question. *Topia: Canadian Journal of Cultural Studies, 12*(Fall), 99–108. https://doi.org/10.3138/topia.12.99

Hylton, M. (2018). The role of civic literacy and social empathy on rates of civic engagement among university students. *Journal of Higher Education Outreach and Engagement 22*(1), 87–106. https://eric.ed.gov/?id=EJ1175772

MacLure, M. (2010). The offence of theory. *Journal of Education Policy, 25*(2), 275–283. https://doi.org/10.1080/02680930903462316

Ricoeur, P. (2004). *Memory, history, forgetting.* University of Chicago Press. https://doi.org/10.7208/chicago/9780226713465.001.0001

The Martin Luther King, Jr. Research and Education Institute. (n.d.). *Steele, Charles Kenzie.* In *The King Encyclopedia.* https://kinginstitute.stanford.edu/encyclopedia/steele-charles-kenzie

Vosloo, R. (2012). Memory, history, and justice: In search of conceptual clarity. *Nederduitse Gereformeerde Teologiese Tydskrif, 53*(3), 215–227. https://doi.org/10.5952/53-0-235

Wilson, A. (2021). Curricularizing social movements: The election of Chicago's first Black mayor as content, pedagogy, and futurities. *Journal of Curriculum Theorizing, 36*(2), 32–42. https://journal.jctonline.org/index.php/jct/article/view/975

Section IV

Act

9   Imagining Civically Engaged Art Education

This project initiated a journey through historical research, community building, and artistic inquiry, which swept us up—educators and students alike—into a process that we have come to understand as civically engaged art education. We began with an intuitive sense of how art education could be more impactful for students, educators, and communities. Since working with the teens on the Foot Soldiers project, we have seen this work develop into a model to help art educators design a curriculum supporting civic agency. In the following chapter, we review students' reflections and conversations by drawing on the exit interviews the teens participated in. As we revisit their words, we discuss how this program supported a three-dimensional model of civic education covering civic knowledge, values, and skills. We also consider how the program was successful in activating cultural production to foster civic capacities. During this analysis, we remain attentive to the definitions of civic reasoning and discourse (Lee et al., 2021) that the National Academy of Education offers to understand the way in which civic capacities show up in educational settings. We close this section with a discussion of how this project evolved our own understanding of how the field of art education can contribute to civic education.

Civic outcomes of the Foot Soldiers program

The summer program started as an exploration of local histories. While we did not explicitly teach toward civic outcomes, we began to see the concept of civics emerge as we analyzed the data at the end of our 2018 program. This was especially apparent in the exit interviews when a student compared her summer experience to her school's civics curriculum.

Sara: Have ya'll learned a lot about civil rights in school?
Kayla: Not a lot.

DOI: 10.4324/9781003199106-13

Viola: I mean, in eighth grade I did, cause this year [11th grade] I took Art History so I didn't have a history class.

Sara: Okay. What did you learn in eighth grade, do you remember?

Viola: Uhm, it was ... the majority of it was like the government. It was [in] civics, so it was like government-related stuff. It wasn't ... I mean there were like some like the Board, like uhm the Board of Education versus Brown.

Sara: The Brown versus Board of Education?

Viola: Yeah, that was like the extent of it.

As we saw students differentiating between the civic knowledge they learned in schools ("government-related stuff"), and the civic values and skills (via the civil rights movement) often absent from those curricula, we made the decision to explicitly focus on the ways this program might introduce and reinforce civic competencies. The differences between the interpretation of civics in our curriculum and what students typically encountered in schools was apparent as we looked closely at how the program engaged students in civic knowledge, values, and skills.

Civic knowledge: Introducing epistemic humility through the work of inquiry

Our program focused exclusively on local history, taking a close look at people, places, and events that impacted Tallahassee. In this Southern capital city, the legacy of the civil rights movement is deep enough to support extensive and nuanced historical research. The disconnect between the wealth of local history we covered in our program and its absence in classroom curriculum unsettled students. When we asked them what surprised them most about our week together, almost every single response mentioned how unaware they had been of the city's past.

Tiffany: This is a small city. I don't want to say it's small but it's, like, quiet and nothing much really happens here. So you wouldn't think that people would do that kind of thing, like that's something for the news. And at least to me, nothing important really happens here on a regular basis.

Kris: I've always just kind of had this vision of Tallahassee as being like, you know, this, like, Podunk town or whatever.

Storm: Saaame!

Kris: It's the Capital or whatever but like it's—

Storm: Boring!

Discovering that history occurred in the place where they were from was deeply meaningful for students. The immediacy of the setting coupled with the access students had to primary source materials helped students confront the fact that history was real. Two students discussed how the archival materials influenced their understanding of history.

Storm: Just knowing like, you know, that these [archival documents] are real, you know that they weren't like, kind of, I don't know how do you say it? Modified to be sugared?

Kris: Yeah, like history sometimes feels like make-believe, like it didn't, like did that actually happen?

Storm: Kind of like how we always, like, learned about Thanksgiving. It was always modified, it was always sugared up, we never really knew the true story until we grew up. And really, just knowing that it was actually from the person's words. They weren't from someone else's mouth, like, sometimes there's biographies but you don't know really if they really said that, you can only read between the lines ... Sometimes researchers don't do their primary sources so you, they read between the lines, between other people's lines, and it gets more faded.

Confronted with primary sources, the students got a sense of history that felt tangible and stood out when compared to the traditional interpretative materials they encountered in K-12 settings. We heard mentions of how materials from their K-12 experiences gave them a sense that history was just a disassociated story, a vague nod to what actually happened. As students began to see how history is constructed through narrative and interpreted by historians, history itself became an object of inquiry. In their investigations, multiple narratives about the civil rights movement emerged, leading students to confront their ahistorical sense of the past.

Kendall: Well for the activists and stuff [who came to visit] it's kind of surprising to me that that happened. Just like, a lot I thought happened a long time ago. But it was a lot more recent than I expected. I never knew there was so many people cuz the way they taught it [the civil rights movement], there's like a few important figures and there's everybody else that just kind of held them up.

These new perspectives shook students' fundamental understanding of history, with insight from our guest speakers pushing their interpretation of history further. In 2019, activist and organizer Bernice Presely mentioned that she had, in fact, been part of the first group of protestors to perform a sit-in at the Woolworth's lunch counter. Because their action did not lead to arrests or any tangible documentation, the story of the local lunch counter sit-ins was simplified to focus entirely on an subsequent sit-in that took place a few weeks later. During this second sit-in, arrests were made and the detainees debuted jail-before-bail tactics, resulting in an outpouring of correspondence and reporting. Student's saw first-hand how history remembers through documents, resulting in the historical forgetting of lived experiences that were never formally documented. The significance of this historical erasure was not lost on students.

Iyawa: I would say that what kind of surprised me, but then not really because like people go unnoticed everyday, was the first group of the people who did the sit-ins, a lot of them aren't recognized. And that's just, like, crazy. ... And I really feel like the first group was as important and if not more important than the second group, because like that's really what got people out the second time, because they saw.

The process of coming to terms with a version of history that lives in the world, outside of textbooks, sets the stage for a powerful civics lesson. Bernice Presley's account of being left out of the historical record illustrated for students that not only are historical narratives selective, but they can also be wrong. Faced with an incomplete record, students were provided the opportunity to become inquirers seeking out missing pieces and historical perspectives. Once students began to move down the path of inquiry, they discovered how complicated this process is. Ava, for example, reflected that when she learned about HBCUs during our visit to the Meek-Eaton Black Archives, she came to a deeper understanding about the depth of history out there, yet to discover:

Ava: I guess I didn't really know that HBCUs were historically important— historically Black colleges & universities. But when I realized how important Florida A&M was, it made me realize that there are places everywhere that will have their own backstory and history that affects the community.

As Ava observed, once you discover the background of one community, you are obliged to consider how easily such stories can multiply as you discover other people and places that have stories to tell. The work the teens engaged in involved taking stock of primary sources, struggling with the trials of constructing and deconstructing historical narratives, and confronting the perpetually unresolved nature of history as ongoing. This work is a lesson about the nature of knowledge. To a certain extent, the knowledge portion of our curriculum was a lesson in epistemic humility, a characteristic that is essential to civics (Warnick, 2022). Coming to terms with the limits of one's own knowledge and understanding the relationship between personal experience and expertise are necessary processes for developing a society that is capable of making collective decisions.

The Foot Soldiers program used creative historical inquiry as a means to introduce a multiplicity of perspectives and competing knowledge claims. This process approximates the nature of civic debates and issues. Lee et al. (2021) characterized civic reasoning as a main outcome of a comprehensive civic education. They defined this skill as the ability to "think through a public issue using rigorous inquiry skills and methods to weigh different points of view and examine available evidence" (p. 1). The Foot Soldier program enacted civic reasoning by having students ask questions and formulate responses. To achieve civic reasoning, students benefit from adopting epistemic humility, which invites them to consider other opinions, not settling on an immediate or unfounded conclusion.

Civic values: Learning to be part of a community

Values are deeply embedded in curriculum and pedagogy. We teach them implicitly and explicitly through the topics we cover, the voices we cite, and the ways in which we establish a relationship with students. As reviewed in Chapter 1, intentional teaching strategies are needed for civic education to avoid potentially contradictory civic models that hinder democratic participation. As Ladson-Billings (2006) reminds us, "no curriculum can teach itself" (p. 33). As we begin this reflection on values, we consider how culturally responsive pedagogy provides a value-oriented framework for teaching democracy. Banks (2017) discussed the importance of this pedagogical approach for developing the skills of participatory citizenship, particularly when working with students with diverse, complex relationships to the nation-state.

Ladson-Billing (2006) observed, while "democracy is a goal for which we are all striving ... for the most part democracy is unevenly and episodically attended to" (p. 39) in schools. This can be problematic for educators, who "are going to have to commit to democracy as a central principle of their pedagogy" (p. 40) regardless of their perceived preparedness to do so. Thus, we are prompted to ask: how can this commitment to democracy materialize? For Ladson-Billings, the answer is not in a set of practices, but an overarching system of values. Ladson-Billings (2006) suggested educators adopt "an ethical position" (p. 40) for teaching toward a better future. While there are tenets that guide culturally responsive pedagogy, at its core this approach requires teachers to "care about the educational futures of their students... and envision them three, five, ten years down the road" (p. 40). This future-oriented approach to teaching that Ladson-Billing described integrates the values of participatory citizenship. In this way, democratic, justice-oriented values become embedded in our teaching when classroom activities are framed as something more than schooling, when curriculum creates opportunities for students to imagine the good life they want to inhabit:

> Although we may only have a yearlong interaction with students, we ultimately have a lifelong impact on who they become and the kind of society in which we will ultimately live.
>
> (Ladson-Billings, 2006, p. 40)

The Foot Soldier program offered a culturally relevant curriculum that started in our local community, and brought the everyday life of our city into alignment with larger narratives about history and current events. We leaned on community members to serve not only as a resource, but as educators in a collective learning process. Lee et al. (2021) suggested that civic reasoning occurs in response to the question, what should we do? Students, however, are not always aware of the collectives they are a part of, and may need opportunities to consider what configurations of "we" include them. Understanding this, the Foot Soldiers program approached civics by attempting to situate students within communities. When we explored how students could begin to see themselves as participatory citizens, we recognized that they may also need to align themselves with a future-oriented project they could be part of.

This shifts our argument to consider that community participation and a sense of belonging are the foundation for developing civic values. Before examining supporting evidence from this project, we must take a moment to recognize that students observed different types of communities when studying the civil rights movement. One such community was characterized by the hostile and terrifying practices of White supremacy:

Sara: What's something that you learned about Tallahassee that you didn't know?

Kayla: Really, just, how big of a thing racism was.

Jada: I guess, how people made them [Black people] feel like they were doing something wrong and they weren't doing anything wrong, they were just walking down the street, and not doing anything.

Iyawa: One thing that I've been thinking about is, like, how a person can hate someone so much that they don't know. Like, you haven't actually met the person and then you, like, hate them? I guess, because of my character, I just can't imagine having so much hate for someone that I would go out of my way to do something to them, to hurt them.

Tiffany: The measures people went through to preserve their perspective on things, like the whole Emmett Till thing. You wouldn't think people would kill a 14-year-old boy just because he was Black.

While confronting racist attitudes that inspired and impacted the work of the civil rights movement, students also observed how individuals and communities harnessed a response to it. We were surprised by the nuance of student reflections. They were not only awed by heroic gestures, but they were also interested in the day-to-day decisions activists made, and what it must have felt like to live with those decisions. For example, Ava grappled with the type of lifelong commitment civic actions demand.

Ava: The civil rights movement *now*, that really surprised me. Plus, those ladies [Gloria Anderson, Bernice Presley] are still working now, I don't think they're retired. I think that's kind of, it's kind of sad. There are people doing all they can, dedicating their entire lives to this. And it's a tedious job ...
[Reflecting on the case file she read on civil rights activist and lawyer Judy Benninger] And, I've seen like the notes and letters she'd [Benninger] written to Patricia Due. And she was saying, like, I want to have, like, a life and everything, but I have to do this and this and this ... Like she was, like, was really going through it, and "I have to keep doing this," and I was like, Oh my god! This is sad. I mean, it takes up so many people's lives. I mean, I knew it was a big deal, but I didn't know, wow like, what they had to actually go through. They were like I need, like, to do this *now*.

Other students reflected on how a deep commitment to a cause leads individuals to make life-altering decisions.

Viola: So, Henry Steele, when I asked him the question if he feared for his life or feared being hurt, uhm ... they [all the activists who chose jail before bail] all decided along with Henry kind of, well, all basically said that it was so important to them that, like, fear wasn't something that was in them. They were just, they were just doing it because it was right and there needed to be a change. So that really, I think during that time a lot of people would have been like "Oh no, we can't do this because so many things could go wrong." But they were fearless in that, and they really believed in what they were doing, so they went up and did it.

We found that the students were deeply impacted by the community they encountered in this project, to the point that they changed how they saw themselves:

Kris: I just feel, like, this week was so important to learn—not just to do art, but like, getting to be with a community of people who are different from myself, to learn about something that wasn't necessarily fun. In a sense, like, you know the civil rights movement is super fascinating and it was super important, but it wasn't necessarily a fun time. Uhm, you know, I just feel like learning about that and being in the setting was so important to me developing who I am as a person, as someone who wants to, wants to help. Even though I'm not, I'm not a person of color and I can't say that I have those experiences. But, I feel like learning about those experiences can help make me a better person and help with the fight, in a sense.

An important conclusion students made was that not only did activism change you, it can also change the community. Students saw the gains made by the civil rights movement, observing how civic action could change minds. Echo shared the following discussion of what she learned:

Echo: I guess how people's viewpoints changed, like from segregation, how they changed their mindset in order to have desegregation.

In response to this observation, Echo made an art project about the mutability of laws, creating a sculpture that emerged out of the middle of a book (see Figure 9.1). Civic participation is built on the belief that your actions are important, that they can lead to change. Echo seemed attuned to this process, and finished the week feeling inspired.

Echo: I don't exactly remember what I wrote down, but it [the final art project] was about how laws change, how they're always changing, and how they affect the people around them.
Sara: And so how are you responding to that?
Echo: I'm doing this paper folding project to show how laws can be dangerous but they are also helpful. And, how they change.

Sara: If I were to take everything that we've done and show other teenagers, what would you hope that they would learn?
Echo: History, like your past, doesn't define you. But it does if you let it.
Sara: Tell me a little bit more about that?
Echo: Because some people have hard times and have a hard time getting over it. And I guess this class has been helpful to me, I think in, like, feeling happier.
Sara: Feeling happier about what?
Echo: Just life in general.

Figure 9.1 Documentation of student work

Using a social movement as curriculum (Ayers et al., 2021) taught students about participatory and justice-oriented citizenship working to advance democratic values. The civil rights movement gave young people a window into the trials, processes, and practices of civic engagement. Of course, given the short duration of the program, our evidence on student impact is limited. However, in the exit interviews, we saw glimmers of evidence suggesting it was successful in embedding democratic values into the curriculum, and thus imparted civic values. The words of these young people at the end of the week suggest that educators should make curriculum not only about the community, but of the community. Studying activism was important, but meeting activists and hearing their memories of political participation seemed to spark something deep in students. Consider how a pair of students vividly recalled an interaction with Annie Harris, a retired educator and assistant superintendent, who welcomed our group into the backyard of her art gallery and home.

Sara: Was the visit to Frenchtown and the Ash Gallery different than what you expected it to be?

Tiffany: Yes. I don't really know what I expected but it was worth going there. It was worth the walk in the heat. It was worth everything.

Sara: What do you think was the most important thing that you got from being there?

Tiffany: Most important thing. All the advice they gave us about—I have a terrible memory. Just the advice in general. And how it's from their own experience, that they know what advice to give us.

Sara: What advice specifically?

Echo: I guess just to help others and help communities.

Tiffany: Yeah, that especially. What fascinated me also was that they were so into just, like, you meet somebody new and you immediately are okay with welcoming them into your house. That's how they are, and then they're like "oh, give me your cell phone number"—

Echo: Yeah, that was so nice.

Tiffany: Give me your cell phone number so if I ever have trouble, or if you ever have trouble, we can call each other and not just meet once and not act like we haven't known each other after a while.

In their talk, Annie Harris and Darryl Scott, shared a message to students about the importance of investing in community. They talked about teaching during desegregation, about later returning to a neighborhood, and the critical role of continuing to serve and invest in that community. They shared about the impact individuals have when committing to the future of their community, they shared a message of connection, collaboration, and comradery. Students heard their message, but what really stuck with them was the invitation to get to know one another, to not let a connection turn into something that just fades away. Of course, we suspect that was precisely what happened, we suspect that Tiffany and Mrs. Harris did not, in fact, call each other. We sense, however, that receiving the invitation was impactful. It was an invitation to Tiffany to stay in touch, to imagine how a moment could extend into a relationship and how these women modeled the values that underlie participatory citizenship.

Civic skills: Artistic responses as the foundation for debate and deliberation

The Foot Soldier program was designed to support both participatory and justice-oriented citizenship. These models involve problem-solving community members who engage, over time, with public-serving institutions, as well as critical interrogators who aim to address and resolve inequities that impact society. Of course, our one-week time frame did not allow us to study in detail the capacity building students developed as a result of their experience in the program. Instead, we turn to the students' art projects, in order to interrogate whether they evidence the civic skills necessary to become a problem solver or critical interrogator.

When we consider what type of civic skills an art classroom may focus on, we return to the national standards presented in the C3 Framework.

> In civics, students learn to contribute appropriately to public processes and discussions of real issues. Their contributions to public discussions may take many forms, ranging from personal testimony to abstract arguments. They will also learn civic practices such as voting, volunteering, jury service, and joining with others to improve society. Civics enables students not only to study how others participate, but also to practice participating and taking informed action themselves.
> (National Council for the Social Studies, 2013, p. 31)

The standards allow for civic skills to align with traditional civic practices that correspond to the rights and responsibilities of citizens. However, the standards also highlight the importance of participating in public discussions. In a similar vein, Lee et al. (2021) offered the concept of civic discourse from which to theorize the application of civic skills. Civic discourse follows the work of civic reasoning, and is defined as the ability to:

> communicate with one another around the challenges of public issues in order to enhance both individual and group understanding. It also involves enabling effective decision making aimed at finding consensus, compromise, or in some cases, confronting social injustices

through dissent. Finally, engaging in civic discourse should be guided by respect for fundamental human rights.

(p. 1)

When civic skills are put to use in *contributing to public discussions* and *communicating about the challenges of public issues* we identify overlaps between art making and civic engagement.

When discussing their final projects, many of our students reflected on how carefully they strived to communicate clearly through their work.

Katie: I also feel, like, as if we're messengers to the public. So, the art-work and creative writing that we're making currently is like a message to the public.

The students were familiar with the task of communicating through art-work, but we were careful to direct the artmaking away from a mode of illustration or representation. We did not want the artwork to mimic im-ages students had come across in their research. Instead, we wanted the artwork to allow students to process, respond to, and share what they had learned. Ruby reflects:

Ruby: Because you guys made us apply it [the artwork] to what's hap-pening now, and our personal lives? That really makes you think. Whenever you think about how it affects you personally, and how it's still going on, it's really difficult to really think about. And you have to learn more, so that you can apply it to your art, and really question yourself on like, what you can do with the knowledge that you have?

The program asked students not just to communicate a message, but to engage in civic discourse alongside their material engagements. This meant that students were continually prompted to name the issue they were fo-cused on, and to think about how their work was contributing to under-standing the issue. Our program did not ask students to make art about the civil rights movement, but to make art about their response to the ongoing legacy of the civil rights movement. As we discussed in Chapter 4, we referenced creative remixing in order to encourage students to engage in a process of deliberation. This is illustrated in Kaylan's mixed media work (see Figure 9.1).

Kaylan: Mine was about how Black Lives Matter and that the Black races are more targeted in life today. Even though back then we

were, like, enslaved but now we are free, but yet we are still being approached all the time.

Rachel: How did you try to communicate that message?

Kaylan: What I used was, I used the Black, African American [abolition-
ist illustration] and he was in shackles. But in the gold banner
below it said that Black Lives Matter and it's supposed to represent hope for the future.

Kaylan's piece reproduces a motif that "became one of the best-known
and enduring of the artistic representations of the abolitionist movement"
(Ditchfield, 2007, para. 3), the widely known 18th-century illustration by
Josiah Wedgwood of a kneeling Black man in slave shackles, raising his
hands toward the sky. This image is often accompanied by a banner with
the question, *Am I not a man and a brother?* In Kaylan's work, the phrase
is replaced with the slogan, Black Lives Matter. In the background, behind
the painting of the abolitionist symbol, Kaylan constructed a brick wall
from collaged paper (see Figure 9.1). The paper she used to make the
bricks was from a print-out of the jail records documenting the arrest of
the participants at the Tallahassee Woolworth's lunch counter sit-in.

Kaylan: I think the hardest part was actually trying to get the message to
be clear in, like, one artwork. Because just looking at it you can't
really tell what you're trying to portray unless you hear a little
bit about it. So that was the hardest part.

Rachel: Okay, so you were worried about people looking at your painting and not knowing what it is about. Is there anything in your
canvas that you think is kind of hard to understand if you don't
know about it?

Kaylan: I believe the bricks are the hardest part because those are actually the jail records of two Foot Soldiers. So, if you don't know
who they are, it's kind of hard to tell what it is.

While Kaylan struggled with conveying her message, we saw potential in
the ambiguous quality of her work. Tracing the connection her work made
between the abolitionist movement, the civil rights movement, and the
Black Lives Matter movement, she framed this piece as hopeful. The difficult imagery of a supplicating man, the muted color tones, and the subject
matter could perhaps lead viewers in a different direction. The point is that
Kaylan succeeded in capturing her response to what she learned during
the week. Her piece was provocative and capable of prompting further
discussion. The conversation that emerged around artworks should not be
discounted, as we saw evidence that the critique process can and should
become a space of debate and deliberation among students. The process

that Ava captured in her reflection below shows how discussing artwork engages students in civic discourse.

Ava: We were offering feedback to everyone, everyone's art project, and there was this girl, and she was like I'm doing—she just drew something, and it was an amazing design—and I was like Oh, I think, it means like this. And then everyone was like well no, it obviously means this, and I was like, Okay. And it kind of, it exposed what they thought about the world which wasn't bad, but it was, it kind of, it was nice to hear what everyone else thought. And, how everyone else felt. And how, since the emotional connection they associated that painting with themselves, it was eye opening to hear the other perspective.

The final comment we will make about communication relates to how some students were prompted to consider their audience, and to consider how their projects may circulate in the public sphere. Aware of the public quality of artwork, Viola clearly considered how her piece might engage the public in understanding and discussing an issue.

Viola: I think the hardest part of mine was trying to get the message across without having it being seen as negative, without other people thinking about it differently than what it's supposed to. So, like, for the doll, I originally wanted them to be Black and White but then I'm like wait, people are going to read that wrong so let's just make it both Black, so I get the point across and not have to have people question why (see Figure 9.1).

During our work with students, we also saw evidence of a shift in their civic agency as a result of their production process. For example, Zoe composed a song and recruited her peers to record it with her. Although it was about the confidence exhibited by groups of activists, it was created with the support of her peers as backup singers. The production of the song became an act of confidence and building a chorus of support. In this way, the process, as much as the content of the piece, was a reflection of civic action.

Zoe: I'm making a song, and most of that was C.K. Steele and how he was boycotting and his quotes. And Millicent Hollifield, and how she was taking care of people with her nursing program. And I put it into a song. When I was reading her bio, it enticed me to keep reading. I liked how she was taking care of people. I would like to do that, too. And C.K. Steele with the buses … if he can do something I can too .... You can do a lot. You don't have to just sit there and watch. You can be out there. Be confident .... You have to keep working to get where you want to be.

Viola, who was working on a message about the choices people made to become activists by painting a portrait of local activist Patricia Stephens Due, also set out to do this work in her own life (see Figure 9.1). So while her connection to action was not attached to the piece literally, the act of making the portrait pushed her to consider how her own voice might be heard.

Viola: There was a quote from Patricia Stephens Due, the one that was "ordinary people can do extraordinary things." We don't have to be like some ... we don't have to be like people who have superpowers or, like, we don't have to be very powerful. We don't have to be like high status to, like, do our part to make a change. We can, even now at this age, we can start making changes, we can go forward and change things in our society, the whole future.

The thinking and making that came out of the Foot Soldier program was a site for documenting students' responses to the legacy of the civil rights movement. The public, dialogic nature of art allowed it to scaffold civic capacities for the students. It served as a way for them to contribute to public discussions, and to work toward the action of advancing understanding around an issue.

Harnessing civic outcomes to design art curriculum

The civic outcomes from the Foot Soldiers project give us an indication that artmaking can support civic knowledge, values, and skills when the curriculum is intentionally oriented toward fostering the capacities of cultural citizens. Lee et al. (2021) emphasized that civic education requires a need for "a more robust and comprehensive form of civic reasoning and discourse education that goes beyond traditional civic education, government, and social studies classes" (p. 398). Contemporary artists have long been embedded in civic reasoning and discourse, using strategies such as political messaging, creative material entanglements, and the art of remixing to suggest ways of being and imagining the world differently. At the same time, socially engaged art trends, critical pedagogies, and the creative multiliteracy practices of participatory youth cultures have influenced the field of art education to move away from traditional, modernist approaches to art production. From our perspective, art education is already doing work that supports civic agency. So, if we become even more intentional in embracing the research on civic education and civic outcomes, alongside contemporary artistic research practices, art education becomes positioned to make a significant contribution to the expansion of civic education for young people.

As evidenced in this chapter, art education can support this challenge by using inquiry to aid students in developing epistemic humility, by creating opportunities for students to become part of something, and by giving time for students' creative outputs to participate in public discourse. If educators can commit to some of these steps, the field will be poised to contribute significantly to young people's civic agency. Pointedly, we do not see this position as relinquishing the art classroom to the purview of other subject areas. Instead, our framing of civically engaged art education explicitly identifies and continues a type of work already underway in the art world. As such, we see the art classroom as a site of deep and meaningful interdisciplinary practice, where students can develop the capacities to shape their communities and their future.

References

Ayers, W., Ayers, R., & Wesheimer, J. (2021). Curriculum of social movements. *Oxford Research Encyclopedias.* https://doi.org/10.1093/acrefore/9780190264093.013.1572

Banks, J. A. (2017). Failed citizenship and transformative civic education. *Educational Researcher*, 46(7), 366–377. https://doi.org/10.3102/0013189X17726741

Ditchfield, M. (2007). Society for the purpose of effecting the abolition of the slave trade. *Oxford Dictionary of National Biography.* https://doi.org/10.1093/ref:odnb/92867

Kahne, J., & Westheimer, J. (2006). The limits of political efficacy: Educating citizens for a democratic society. *PS: Political Science & Politics*, 39(2), 289–296. https://doi.org/10.1017/s1049096506060471

Ladson-Billings, G. (2006). "Yes, but how do we do it?" Practicing culturally relevant pedagogy. In J. Landsman & C. W. Lewis (Eds.), *White teachers/diverse classrooms: A guide to building inclusive schools, promoting high expectations, and eliminating racism* (pp. 29–42). Stylus Publishing.

Lee, C. D., White, G., & Dong, D. (2021). *Educating for civic reasoning and discourse.* National Academy of Education. https://naeducation.org/educating-for-civic-reasoning-and-discourse/

NCSS (National Council for the Social Studies). (2013). *College, career & civic life (C3) framework for social studies state standards: Guidance for enhancing the rigor of K-12 civics, economics, geography, and history.* National Council for the Social Studies. https://www.socialstudies.org/system/files/2022/c3-framework-for-social-studies-rev0617.2.pdf

Warnick, B. R. (2022). Epistemic humility and democratic education. In, J. Culp, J. Drerup, I. de Groot, A. Schinkel, & D. Yacek (Eds.), *Liberal democratic education: A paradigm in crisis* (pp. 83–100). Brill Mentis. https://doi.org/10.30965/9783969752548_006

Westheimer, J., & Kahne, J. (2004). What kind of citizen? The politics of educating for democracy. *American Educational Research Journal*, *41*(2), 237–269. https://doi.org/10.3102/00028312041002237

10 Designing Curriculum

The Foot Soldier summer program contemplated the legacy of the civil rights movement in Tallahassee, Florida and considered how a combination of activities such as thinking like historians, making like artists, and working within communities could allow students to craft an inclusive, collective memory of historical events. By engaging with history through archives, artifacts, community members, and the shifting urban landscape, we confronted the ways through which history is carried into and sustained in the present. This work invited students to situate themselves within this emerging timeline, in relation to their community and their community's future. While these were the goals of our program, we want to introduce ways of establishing your own outcomes and harnessing the potential of your community as you adapt this project to fit your own context. Thus, the aim of this chapter is to provide tools and strategies for others to research, plan and develop their own civically engaged art curricula.

This chapter offers a pragmatic discussion around curriculum development that includes a series of prompts, questions, activities, and steps to follow, as you develop a civically engaged art curriculum that is locally situated, contextually relevant, and culturally and politically responsive. In this chapter, we challenge you to work toward developing a curriculum that places students' lived experiences and relationships with their communities at the center. Of particular interest in this chapter is the notion of community, as it serves to connect your own curriculum development with the prior sections. As you move through these curriculum spirals, we ask you to think with local histories, make with contemporary, culturally relevant artists, and act as an invested community member.

Thinking with local histories

Viola: I would really say, like, for teachers to really talk about things that are happening in the place you live. Cause I feel like it's really

DOI: 10.4324/9781003199106-14

important to know what happened in Tallahassee for us, cause we live here, and to know all that history is really important. Like history in general is important but like to really know where we're from, our history is really important.

In our exit interviews with students we asked them to share what they thought was the best way for teachers to use this approach in their classrooms. As you read in Chapter 9, students indicated an overwhelming interest in learning about their communities. Using this feedback as a touchstone, we wonder what a classroom that responds to the local might look like in a K-12 context. Thinking back to the discussion on place-based pedagogy in art education (see Chapter 3), we see how this curricular model opens up opportunities for young people to learn about their communities' varied cultural influences. We recall the discussion of civic ecosystems from Chapter 3, where we posit that schools might serve as central locations in the complex web of cultural, social, political, and ecological perspectives making up the civic ecosystem (Blandy, 2011; Childs, 2001). If this is the case, then it becomes the obligation of the school, and thus the teachers, to fold in a variety of perspectives representing the communities students belong to. But to be able to teach students to engage in their communities, educators must first learn about these communities. Educators should do the work of excavating their community's local history through engagement with physical places, primary documents, and a combination of traditional and creative methods of place-based inquiry. We take this moment to note that, for our context, history became a cornerstone of this investigation, but this need not be interpreted as a one size fits all model. Pressing issues facing your community in the present— e.g., immigration, climate change, gentrification and so on—may be better suited to contextualize and personalize your curriculum. Mainly, we ask teachers to find their own glowing data (MacClure, 2010, 2020) within their community and consider that as a starting point for their curricular development. As you move through the subsequent sections, we invite you to write in the margins, take a walk, and do the work necessary to think through how your curriculum might respond to the world around you.

Learning with(in) places

Iyawa: We focus so much on other places, not where we are right now, where we live. Why don't we talk about it now? I mean it's okay to talk about other places, but we live here and so much has happened.

To begin your focused community investigation, you might first take some time to identify what you already know about your community.

We suggest taking some time to make a list, write, or draw about your community. While you are engaged in this, remember that a community can be a physical place, group of people, institution, or any grouping that shares a common denominator. As you think about what you know, think about how that knowledge is situated in the place you, your school, and your students live in. It is also critical to think about the communities you have access to. These communities should be relevant to you, your school, and your students. As you make your list, consider which of these communities stands out. Is it a neighborhood? A local organization? A group? Why does the community stand out? Think carefully about which community you might want to learn more about. This is a critical step because in this consideration you must think about both your own interest (which is central to this kind of teaching) and the interests of your students. We also caution you to be thoughtful in considering what your students might want to learn about. We were surprised to learn from the young people that we worked with that they perceived teachers as consistently underestimating their capabilities.

Now it is time to engage in a scavenger hunt of sorts. Visit the places you think are significant to your community history. Find information by doing research online or talking with community members. Begin to build an archive (digital or physical) that contains what you learned about and experienced in your community. This archive can include screenshots, photographs, articles, lists of historical sites and monuments, videos, interviews, personal memories, documentation from site visits, or stories (both historical and oral). Allow yourself to follow the rabbit hole, investigate what intrigues you, listen to oral histories, read newspaper articles, do whatever it takes to immerse yourself in the ephemera of the community.

As you learn more, be sure to chart your reflections on how your thinking has changed. Has your relationship to places in your community changed? How did your research impact this relationship? We suggest moving through iterations of researching and reflecting several times. We also encourage you to routinely visit the places that come up in your research. The work you are doing now will set the groundwork for the investigation you invite your students into, so taking the time to really immerse yourself is critical. This kind of investigation might be best done over a summer break, when you have some time and energy to get out and do some digging. After you have cycled through several iterations of researching, visiting places, and uncovering local histories, compile a resource list. This list should include websites that were helpful in gathering information, notes on how you accessed archival information, and any place (both actual and virtual) that was helpful in finding out more about your community. Take your time on this, as this resource will become a tool for your students to do their own investigations later.

Curriculum prompting

1 Create two to three essential questions related to the place and events you have researched so far
2 Consider what outcomes students will achieve by thinking/exploring/ researching the essential questions
3 Reflect on how you will know they have met these outcomes

Making with(in) places

At the end of this personal investigation into community histories, you'll likely find yourself gravitating toward a story, a person, a historical account, or some other glimmer. The next phase of the curriculum design process involves digging into this glimmer to find your way to the starting point for your curriculum project. We have found that the next step of the process needs something tangible to move out of; for us, places served as a touchstone. We suggest that you start by asking yourself: what place or location stands out to you from your research and reflections? Write this place down and commit to doing something with the place. Think back to the exercise we asked our students to engage in, where they collected photographs and rubbings from many of the key locations we explored in our trips around Tallahassee. How might you use this prompting to create something of your own? This is not a high-stakes making experience, rather it is the opportunity to slow down and spend time in a location that holds your interest. Think of this as a get-to-know-you exercise, where you are tasked with creatively responding to the place that you identified at the end of your research. The creative response can take many forms: photographs, collage, poetry, journaling, video documentation of a visit, a map (from memory or observation), a painting, sketch, or even sculpture. Do something with the place, engage and experience it, try using the creative activity to shift your perspective.

As art teachers we often ask our students to do "projects" but rarely do we engage in our own investigations of the topic. We see this process of making with places as critical to the next steps of the curriculum. Just as you will be asking your students to engage in arts-based inquiry practices, so should you engage in artmaking experiences that are driven by learning, not by outcomes. Try to engage in the creative process of getting to know the place, without recreating or representing the place. Stop yourself throughout the process and ask what is working, what isn't working, what is exciting, what are you not enjoying, what moves you, what stalls you. Take note of how you respond to these questions and use these notes to guide you into the next phase of the curriculum design spiral, where we move from local places, to the events that unfold(ed) in those places.

Making with artists

Kris: So art is a reflection of one's world, one's culture. It kind of shows your life, your experience, all the things that are important to you. Uhm, so you know, when historians gather up art from history it actually can tell something about that period of time. Uhm, for example, you know, we don't know a whole lot about a lot of ancient cultures except from what we've learned from their art ... Uhm so yeah, it's really important to learn from art, because it's a reflection of history.

As you look back on your thinking and making from the previous stage, begin to recap what you learned about your local community's history through your creative inquiry into a physical place. How does your place contribute to the civic ecosystem of your community? Your school community? Your students' community? Remember, that civic ecosystems rely on places and respond to how people interact in them, they are made of a complicated flow of ideas, resources, and relationships. As you unpack the role of place in your civic landscape, you are also likely beginning to see how that place—and the history it holds—has been either celebrated, remembered, or even forgotten. By always looking backward and forward, at the way places have been celebrated, remembered, or erased, your curriculum moves between then and now, exploring history as a series of events that are still impacting and unfolding in the present.

This program holds a unique space for the consideration of art. This approach addresses the important role of art by noting the incompleteness of history, the impermanence of places, and the imperfections of interpretations. Contemporary artists document ongoing histories in an effort to participate in the present. Therefore, your curriculum can (and should) respond to the complicated nature of history by considering how artists and art might do some of the work of filling these voids. For this next phase of curricular planning, we ask you to look at how the work of contemporary artists can teach us about the event of making art, inviting you to consider how artmaking interacts with the development of historical events and narratives. This focus recognizes the important role of art in activating participation and moving students through inquiry. We suggest artmaking and artistic inquiry as a foundation for considering how art works as a valuable tool in a civically engaged curriculum.

We begin this spiral, by asking you to join us as we engage the work of several contemporary artists that have been referenced throughout this volume. These artists were important because they taught us about how artistic inquiry could remix, reimagine, and reframe historical narratives. While these artists make deeply impactful and evocative work, we chose them because they were engaged in the process of making with history through their artistic practices. Essentially, these artists engaged in practices that mirrored the ways we wanted the students at our summer experiences to work. So while these artists serve as an illustrative example for our own project, they may not be the right artists for your curriculum. With that in mind, we also guide you to actively work on expanding your own artist repertoire to include artists that are making with themes that support your community and students. During this investigation, we encourage you to locate and get to know local artists that are thinking with the local and making with your community.

Reimagining history: Kevin Beasley

Kevin Beasley uses iconic, historic images to reimagine narratives of power and authority. In both our summer programs we referenced Beasley's large-scale installation, *Chair of the Ministers of Defense*. This work recreates the *Cathedra Petri* with contemporary symbols from Black culture, while referencing the iconic peacock chair that Huey P. Newton, leader of the Black Panthers, sat in. We paired visuals of this work with the Hammer Museum's interview of Beasley, which asks the question "What does it mean to replace Bernini's *Chair of Saint Peter* with the chair of Huey P. Newton?" (Hammer Projects: Kevin Beasley, n.d.). We chose Beasley's work because of his close connection with archival images and references to classic artforms, like the altarpiece. Like other contemporary artists, Beasley expertly draws on references from art and history, connecting them to a present-day iconography. Beasley's work highlights the way in which contemporary art connects students to primary sources through material engagements. We see this influence in the work of students like Dwayne, who utilized the classic form of a triptych to remember and recognize what being a young Black man in America has looked like throughout history (for details of Dwanye's work see Chapter 6).

Remixing narratives: Willie Cole

Willie Cole uses objects from everyday life to create prints and assemblages that remix the past with his own experiences (Willie Cole, n.d.). We specifically referenced *Domestic I.D. IV* (1992), *American Domestic* (2016), and *Five Beauties Rising* (2012) in the two summer programs. All three of these pieces contain a reference to irons and ironing boards, an object that when printed or burned onto a surface feels eerily reminiscent of birdseye diagrams of slave ships (see Blake, 1860, p. 304) and African tribal masks. We chose Cole's work because of how he uses objects to reference historic and archival imagery, as well as his own experiences being raised by a mother and grandmother who worked as housekeepers. The work remixes imagery of tribal masks, slave ships, and his family history, to speak to the impact the enslavement of Africans has in our contemporary world. His work relies on the centrality of objects in holding and teaching us about history. This work resonated with many of our students who were inspired by the visit to the Meek-Eaton Black Archives and Museum, where students like Viola encountered objects, like the topsy-turvy doll, that later became the focus of their own artistic investigations, remixing archival objects/imagery with their own life experiences (for details of Viola's work see Chapter 7).

Reframing the future: Favianna Rodriguez

Favianna Rodriguez harnesses the power of narrative in politics and political movements. Her work as a printmaker engages the history of anti-immigration policies in the United States. Having researched how shifts in social understandings lead to changes in policy, Rodriguez's art and activism is geared toward impacting how society views migration. In the pursuit of meaningful change through immigration policy reform, Rodriguez designs posters, shirts, and graphics, all while organizing community events that call for change. We chose Rodriguez because of the explicit connections her work has to the important role the arts can play in reimagining civic life. Rodriguez frames her work through a "yes" framework. In an environment where activism is often engaged in resistance—or saying no—her artmaking locates a particular power for contributing rather than negating. Combining artmaking and activism, Rodriguez is a guide for how the work of art can move toward action through the use of visionary artistic practices, bringing communities into a conversation about change. We see echoes of Rodriguez's influence in work like Zoe's (see Chapter 7), where Zoe used the format and history of a protest song to encourage her community to continue the work of activism today.

Revisiting events and the role of contemporary art

These artists served as touchstones for our program. By making with history, they illustrated how the contemporary art world is doing the same kind of work that we were asking the young people in the Foot Soldiers program to engage in. We were careful to select artists whose work was approachable and looked like it could be within a sphere of possibility for young artists. For example, we could have easily used work by Kehinde Wiley instead of Kevin Beasley, but worried that the technical nature of Wiley's work may leave even the most talented artists feeling unsuccessful. In our program, we made conscientious decisions to use artists that create non-representational work, as we were interested in processes that could invite students to bring in materials found or created during their research process. Ultimately, we wanted to open up possibilities for artmaking that were not from the traditional canon of *projects* in art classrooms, thus we chose to not use artists who relied heavily on painting or drawing competencies. This was a choice we made due to the time restrictions in our projects, which is not a choice that all teachers must make.

What is important for the next stage of curriculum planning is that you do the work of expanding your own repertoire of contemporary artists. Remember that this repertoire should represent a range of demographics and present multiple models of what artmaking can look like. At this stage, revisit your research from the first curriculum spirals, and continue by working from the ground up, realizing that while places may ground the beginning of your curricular conversation, they also serve as an invitation to study the things that happen in those spaces.

We now invite you to extend this thinking to consider how your curriculum might impact the trajectory of the events in the future. For us, our place was downtown Tallahassee, the event was the civil rights movement, and the future orientation of the project was to recognize how community members made valuable and necessary contributions to social movements. We saw our curriculum as offering opportunities for students to see, identify, and explore historic and contemporary sites of social/political organizing and resistance. We wanted to find ways to honor, recognize, and highlight these locations by exploring with teens what organizing has looked like in their own community. We wanted to use our curriculum to explore the everydayness of social movements, by establishing an understanding that these events require daily commitment and planning, that the work of making change is ongoing, requiring teamwork, focus, and commitment.

Like the curriculum covered in this volume and the artists reviewed in this chapter, the historical event and its contemporary relevance will serve as a starting point for your own investigation of contemporary artists. As you, and your students, engage in artmaking, we remind you that should be a complex site for inquiry, reflection, and creative imagining. In this way, artmaking moves the project forward, referencing the sites and documents of research while making space for a reflection on the impact of historical events and a vision of the possibilities for the future.

After you identify an event, we ask you to identify an artist whose work engaged these events or places. Learn about the artist by doing a deep dive into their work. Like you did in the earlier spiral, keep an archive of this learning. Find a place to record the websites, videos, images, and interviews that you encounter in your research process. As your investigation moves, ask yourself how learning about places and events through the artist might engage your students. Will students make connections with the mediums or messages? Will the work make them feel or understand something? Will the work highlight a process or represent an alternative viewpoint? Continue to follow this thinking and identify more artists, ideally an artist that represents a different relationship with curriculum than the other(s). This stage of the planning process is critical, because the artists you select will set the stage for the kinds of inquiry you want your own students to engage in. we recommend creating a repertoire of at least five contemporary artists whose work is approachable for students and who use themes or processes related to your place and/or event. As you learn about artists, we want you to begin to shift to a consideration of action, which sets the stage for the final spiral in our curriculum process.

Curriculum prompting

1 How does your teaching (learning about places and events) empower your students?
2 How does art cause disruption?
3 How might the curriculum cause disruption?
4 How do you think about curriculum as a visionary project, one that might plant a seed and develop practices over outcomes?
5 How does art support the curriculum as a visionary project?

Acting as community members

As you begin to get an understanding of the potential for engaging in curricular explorations of events unfolding inside of your community, you also can think about what the space of action is for your students and what might be missing from that space of action. Do you work at a school where students have staged walkouts, like students in South Florida did in 2022, in response to the passage of the Parental Rights in Education Bill, nicknamed the *Don't Say Gay Bill*; or have your students participated in organized events outside of the school, like cleaning up a local river or park; or maybe your students have no experience with these models of civic participation, but like most teenagers find opportunities to share their ideas about the world in social media spaces through hashtag activism. How can these spaces for participation, in the school, the community, or social media, provide opportunities to ground conversations about civic action? Maybe, like many teachers, you work in a school that is actively working against teacher autonomy, maybe your school library is being overturned and inspected, or your lesson plans are being highlighted and scrutinized. These spaces offer opportunity for action as well, and might best be suited for projects where the community is the school, and the space of action is just in your classroom. What is important, is not that the action reverberates far, but that action happens, allowing students to respond to the question: what should we do?

As you consider the sphere of action for your students, you can recall the places and events from earlier spirals. You might want to consider how your place introduced you to events that connect your community to civic activities or how events (historical or contemporary) shape your community as a civic space. By staring at the local, through the access points of places and events, you can communicate to your students what civics is and how it shapes your unique community. This begins a spiral of thinking that invites students to consider how local places manifest civic activity and how you and your students might become a part of it.

Contributing through art

> *Activism –> Effect*
> *Art –> Affect*
> At first glance [art and activism] seem at odds with one another. Activism moves the material world, while art moves a person's heart, body, and soul. The scope of the former is social, while the latter is individual. In fact, however, they are complimentary. The social is not some mere abstraction; society is composed of people, and change does not just happen. It happens because people make change. As such, the individual and the social are intertwined. … That is to say: before we act in the world, we must be moved to act.
> (Parenthesis added; Duncombe, 2016, pp. 216–217)

Drawing on projects developed within the Center for Artistic Activism, Duncombe (2016) introduces a list of outcomes of activist art (see Box 10.1). Using this list, he offers a framework for understanding how art *works*, or how it impacts the world. We did not connect this project to Duncombe's activist art outcomes until after we concluded our summer programs. As we met regularly to review our data and planned the next steps for our research and curriculum development, we sought out ways to align the civics framework from Chapter 1 with the work that we saw the students producing. While there were clear lines connecting the work with the civic knowledge, values, and skills, there was something more happening that was directly related to the art itself, and we struggled to articulate it. As we reviewed the project documentation, we observed that the way these young people talked about themselves, their community, and their learning, evoked deep emotions that presented evidence of civic capacities, but they also seemed to do something else.

Box 10.1 Activist Art Outcomes

Foster Dialogue: creating a conversation, usually around uncomfortable or overlooked topics.

Build Community: building and maintaining community.

Make a Place: creating places where discussions happen and communities meet, and where novel ways of thinking, being, and creating can be explored, tested, or lived

Invite Participation: turning watchers into doers.

Transform Environment and Experience: altering people's environmental experiences and bodily practices.

Reveal Reality: holding up a mirror to reflect an aspect of the world otherwise unseen, and/or provide factual information about an issue that is little known.

Alter Perception: changing the way people perceive reality. One of the powers of art is its ability to help us to see the world through new eyes

Create Disruption: disrupting business-as-usual. Disruption can be cultural: challenging how people commonly think about an issue, or material; disturbing how things are usually done.

Inspire Dreaming: visualizing, either literally or figuratively, an alternative world.

Provide Utility: creating a useful tool.

Political Expression: expressing one's political feelings.

Encourage Experimentation: conducting an ongoing experiment.

Maintain Hegemony: perpetuating the powers-that-be.

Make Nothing Happen: not "working" at all. Perhaps one believes that the biggest problem of contemporary society is that everything has to have a function.

Duncombe's activist art outcomes helped us, and we hope you, reframe what action means. In wrapping up our project, we struggled to reconcile the role of action when most of our students engaged in traditional artmaking that seemed to start and stop at the end of the week. What we cannot know, as we discussed in Chapter 9, is whether this work stretches beyond the confines of a weeklong program. What are the long-term outcomes of this kind of work with young people? How does it change their ability to be engaged in the civic landscape of their communities? Does this work, as we posit in Chapter 4, help foster attachments to community and will those attachments turn into investment, which manifests as engagement? This is where Duncombe's (2016) writing on the so-called "æffective" capabilities of artwork began to build a bridge between what we felt and what we knew as art educators. This list of outcomes captures how the work of making and looking at art moves us, and when that work is about the place you call home, perhaps that movement becomes engagement, and that engagement, one day, fosters change.

For this closing spiral of our curriculum development guide, we ask you to consider how art *works* by impacting the community. We took time to map Duncombe's activist art outcomes over a matrix cataloging intellectual, participatory, and dispositional civic outcomes. What emerged has been a helpful tool in making decisions about how to engage in the final steps of designing a civically engaged art curriculum. We suggest that you might want to take some time to create a map that charts connections and overlaps between these two frameworks (see Table 10.1). To do this mapping exercise you might consider the following questions:

1 What are the specific dispositions that lead to the actions needed to make change?
2 What outcomes from the civics framework are missing in the activist art outcomes and what art outcomes are missing from the civics framework?

Centering people

Now that you have mapped the art outcomes alongside the civic outcomes, we challenge you to return to the events you identified earlier. As you center events, and the places that held them, we ask you to consider how people embody places, events, and history. This step was perhaps the most critical in our own curriculum development; we found that introducing case files of individual participants in the civil rights movement invited strong responses and engagement from students. The centrality of people is critical for working with young people, who do not have a full understanding of the complex and layered ways that history has played out. When viewing local communities and events we asked the teens to follow the story of the people that participated in them. We challenge you to think of how you might ask young people to associate a face and a name with an event or a place. There is power in this process. We saw this in the work with the young people in our program; we observed when Dwayne saw a boy, just a few years older than him, who gave his life to register voters; when Iyawa saw her own heritage in the stories of a boy and his father who chose to start a movement; when Viola interrogated her own identity as a Black girl being raised by White parents; and when Zoe heard the voices of her peers in the songs of community resistance.

Table 10.1 Matrix for civic engagement

Civic Capacities		
Intellectual (knowledge)	*Participatory (skills)*	*Dispositional (values)*
Critical thinking	Engaging in dialogue with those who hold different perspectives	Tolerance, respect, and appreciation of difference
Perspective taking	Active listening	Desire for community involvement
Understanding, interpreting, and critiquing various media	Communicating and voicing opinions through public speaking, letter writing, petitioning, canvassing, lobbying, protesting (non-electoral means)	Rejection of violence
Understanding, interpreting, and critiquing different points of view	Managing, organizing, participating in groups	Concern with the rights and welfare of others
Expressing one's opinions	Organizing and demonstrating	
	Building consensus and forging coalitions	Commitment to balancing personal liberties with social responsibility to others
Active listening	Community mapping	Personal efficacy and attentiveness to civic matters
Identifying public problems	Utilizing electoral processes	Sense of belonging to a group or party
Drawing connections between democratic concepts and principles and one's own life experience	Planning and running meetings	Readiness to compromise personal interests to achieve shared ends
	Utilizing strategic networks for public ends	

As you identify people, think of the kids you teach, and find people that reflect them in some way. Are they similar in age? Do they share the same religion? Did they grow up in the same neighborhoods? Do their skin colors match? Did they attend the same school? As you ask students to investigate the people, places, and events of your community, highlighting connections between the people of the past and the students of the present is critical. Even more important is taking the time to get to know these people, reach out to interview them, or just invite them for a coffee. Attend a church service or a gallery opening. Stop in and listen to a lecture or participate in a community event. You do not have to do all these things at once, but you might find that once you start, you will not want to stop. Once you get a working list of people (both historic and contemporary) return to the map of civic and art outcomes, and think about what dispositional traits these people share with the list. How do these people demonstrate the kinds of civic disposition impacting action? What dispositions could you bring into your classroom?

Curriculum prompting

1 Essential Questions:

   a Do your EQs relate to the people in your community (historic/present)?
   b Are these questions investigatory?
   c How do your questions relate or embed the civic dispositions?
   d How do your questions relate or embed artistic dispositions?
   e How can you re-write to develop your questions more?

2 Learning Outcomes:

   a Workshop the learning outcomes to align them with civic skills and activist artistic outcomes.
   b Consider what needs to be done in your school.
   c Identify what you can do with students and how art can contribute to that.
   d Explore how these collective actions can start to get you to the place you imagined.

Thinking | Making | Acting through curriculum design

So far this chapter has asked you to learn about community and begin working through curriculum design. You have spiraled through a process of beginning to think with local communities, by identifying local places that hold relevance to your community. You have begun to consider the ways you might take inspiration from contemporary artists, in order to make art that dialogues with historic and contemporary events that have unfolded in your communities. Finally, you have connected these places and events with key people from your community and identified what qualities these people possess that overlap with artistic and civic outcomes. Essentially, you have created a stockpile of curricular resources unique to you, your students, and your community. Now you can take these disparate parts and piece them together into a framework for your own students to work inside of. As you revisit your research with your students in mind, we wanted to remind you of a few resonate qualities from our own project that young people have identified as helpful or necessary in the process of becoming arts-based researchers. To present these ideas, we offer you a tangible suggestion we have positioned alongside the voices of our students. As you consider these suggestions, we hope that you read their words, hear their voices, and recognize your own students in them.

Lean into the hard

Viola: I really like how open you guys are to just talk. So you guys are not afraid to, like, bring up any topic and have us talk about it. And although there will be people in the class that won't agree, you guys aren't afraid to just bring those topics out and have us talk about it.

Don't be afraid to ask students to look at the hard parts of the world. This rang true in our own investigations with the teens in the Foot Soldiers program. Recall, in the illustrative case studies, our initial hesitancy to take kids into part of the Meek-Eaton Black Archives, or show the footage from the Emmett Till case. Ultimately, we made the decision to allow the teens to make choices about what they wanted to view. Instead of assuming that it was too much for them, we leaned into the hard history of the Black struggle for freedom, and we gave the teens the power to opt-in and -out of activities. Consistently we were surprised by the teens' willingness to engage in these hard histories with a critical eye. It is telling that much of the information that was difficult to read or see became the impetus of students' artmaking. Students rose to the challenge of asking difficult questions and we saw that, more than anything, young people craved to be trusted with this level of responsibility.

Get out of the classroom

Storm: Can we go to the national archive?
Storm: Let's go get buried under like all the paper.
Kris: Give me all of the newspapers, give me all of them.
Storm: Dude, you like literally love those newspapers. Yeah, like, just seeing all those papers and actually touching them it's like a big fact of history.
Kris: I didn't expect to get so excited.

We know this is hard, but getting students out into the community became a central theme in conversations about what the teens wanted to do more of, in schools. Think about how you can upend the daily classroom routine. Maybe you can't physically leave campus, but can you leave your classroom? Leaving the structure and environment of the physical space of the classrooms immediately opens up opportunities for students to do and think differently. We have conditioned young people to think that school is where learning occurs, but for our students the school and classroom were not where learning happened, but where learning commenced. We want to encourage you to apply for the grant, reach out to local organizations, and visit those people and places you discovered in your early work on your curriculum. You never know if someone might be willing to offer support, or pitch in by bringing their story or place into your classroom.

Ask questions

Dwayne: Well you know, you guys are willing to give your opinion and receive others. Like yeah, that's pretty good

Iyawa: Also, something I really like is that if someone has an idea, you guys were like: go with it. You're like, asking more questions about it instead of being like, no you can't do that.

Asking questions seems like an obvious part of designing a curriculum, but when we talked with the teens at the end of the summer program we heard this come up, over and over. Young people want to be listened to, they want their ideas considered, and they want to feel like their teacher is invested in them. We believe this is best achieved through asking questions. We don't mean questions about meeting objectives—"what are you doing?" "what next," "why did you do that." Instead, we mean questions that invite collaboration, future engagement, and mutual attention. The beauty of this model is that you don't have to be the only one asking questions, when you start to facilitate a space of inquiry, you will find that students will begin to ask each other questions. As you design your own curriculum, intentionally scaffold in question asking. This may start with a critique or exit ticket, but when used with regularity and consistency, students will come to anticipate questions and eventually begin asking their own.

Invite the community in

Iyawa: It's different when you have a person that went through it, sitting down there, talking to you, because it kind of feels like you went back in time when they're telling you the stuff. It's like they're there if you touch them.

Inviting in the community was deeply impactful for our students. As we think back on our own invitations for community participation via visits to our classroom, we reflect that this was perhaps one of the easiest parts of designing our projects. While we often sent that first email with a little trepidation, we were almost always met with an enthusiastic response.

People want to share their stories. Giving someone the opportunity to share is often as much of a gift to them as it is for your students. We found that utilizing social media and local news outlets proved to be the most useful ways for contacting individuals. Early in this chapter, we asked you to list people that were relevant to this inquiry. This is the chance to revisit that list and reach out to people, you too might be surprised at the stories your community wants to share with you and your students.

Foster autonomy

Iyawa: Maybe, giving us a decision of what we want to do
Mona: Instead of just telling us right away.
Iyawa: Yeah, like give us a general topic, and then we research and pick what we want to do.
Mona: Not just like, everybody does the same thing, and whoever does it better gets the better grade. We do different things, like how we did here. Everybody has a different point of view.

This too seems obvious, especially in an art room, but giving students autonomy is not enough, instead you have to teach them how to be autonomous. Remember that most students have spent their entire student careers being taught how to listen, asked to follow directions, and told when to answer them. When we foster autonomy in our students, we invite them into a process where there is no right answer, instead we provide the necessary structure for students to develop their own course of action. This model is not complete autonomy, but instead introduces, develops, and sharpens the skills necessary to be an independent thinker. For us, the field guides were how we did this. We created multiple opportunities for students to respond to the experiences we encountered together. Importantly, we didn't require that they complete a certain number of pages or specific prompts, instead we gave them the resource and asked them to use it as they needed it. Within a framework that prompted inquiry and reflection, students were able to develop a process they recognized themselves in.

Center students

Ava: You know, you hear kids say all the time, what in the world that's got to do with me? Why am I sitting here for four hours and then I'm going to forget it in, like, two days! You know, I think if you find a way to relate it to the students, especially like this, how a lot of this is related to my history and everything, wow a lot of it is related to my history! I mean it was really interesting! Like, I got here. I woke up Monday morning at like 5:45!

This is another curricular quality that feels obvious for art teachers, but often gets misinterpreted in practice. By asking you to center students, we are not asking you to necessarily ask students questions like "who are you?" Instead, we suggest that you provide a curriculum that constantly invites students to view what they are learning through the lens of themselves. This was another useful quality of the field guides, where we frequently asked students to relate what they saw to something from their own lives. We also did this by including voices from community members, historic figures, and artists that our students could identify with. This did not entail checking a box that aligns with every demographic in your class, but rather designing a curriculum that invited students to inquire into their communities as they searched for their own place of belonging.

Reinforce trust

Theo: Freedom, you guys gave us freedom. Teachers don't give us freedom. They don't even let us just get up and go to the bathroom, they don't trust us ... You feel more loose, you don't have to be all tied up like you're going to get in trouble or something.

Listen, we know you can't just let students go to the bathroom whenever they want to, but we also know that isn't what Theo is really talking about. What Theo, and others, recognized in the summer program was that we didn't prescribe the outcome of the work. When we started the week, no one in the room knew where they would end up. This is the kind of freedom that Theo is speaking to. We trusted that students would find their own entry points and gave students chances to find their own way. We asked students what they needed from us, instead of just telling them what we needed from them. We constantly reminded them that this week was about their city, their interests, and ultimately their journey to become engaged community members. The freedom that Theo refers to is not just physical freedom, but intellectual and artistic freedom. This kind of freedom can only be achieved through mutual trust and respect. You have to go into your classroom truly believing that your students and community have something to teach you, and then you have to practice trusting that you'll find it together.

Designing a civically engaged art education curriculum

A civically engaged art curriculum is built around pedagogical relationships. We found that it was essential to position students as researchers if we were working toward the dispositional outcomes of civic agency. Turning your classroom into a space for student research does not mean teachers no longer teach. Instead, this process entails bringing into your classrooms a sophisticated act of research in practice. Perhaps the saying "those who can, do, and those who can't, teach" holds some truth. Those who can do, and they do with their students—they work with their students to foster creative capacities and develop the skills, tools, and processes necessary to conduct independent inquiry practices. When students are asked to go out into the world, ask questions, meet community members, follow ideas that spark individual interests, and are trusted to engage in autonomous investigations that bring in the critical and creative capacities of the arts, classroom learning becomes relevant to their lives. This model of curriculum engenders a care for community that we saw in both students' individual art explorations and in their closing interviews at the end of the Foot Soldiers program. We have discussed, elsewhere in this volume, that care for community yields attachment to place, thus laying the groundwork for civic engagement (Stefaniak et al., 2017). When art classrooms become the site for these investigations, then art teachers are tasked with designing curricular opportunities that engender imagination and wonder. Such experiences can lead young people into wider relation with the world, prompting them to consider a central question of civics: what should we do to make the world better? (Lee et al., 2021)

This question of "what should we do" reinforces civics education's aim of fostering the capacity for young people to build and sustain the public sphere. This is also a question asked from within the arts, as contemporary artists seek ways to comment on and impact the social and political worlds they live in. When looking at the contemporary art world, we can observe how the work of art manifests through modes of æffective civic participation, where artists reference knowledge about policy, laws, and rights; evoke values related to democracy, liberalism, and the "good life;" and activate creative and civic skills to make real change in our communities. We wonder then, as society consistently turns to public education to serve as a centralizing force that works in support of democracy, why the art classroom is not recognized as a site for the types of thinking, making, and acting that support civic engagement. As schools continue to underperform in civics, why are school systems not pursuing alternative models of civic education? Most educators already know the answer: schools acutely feel the repercussions of the systemic inequities that shape society in this country. These are the very problems civic education is tasked with solving. An unequal distribution of resources, the persistence of exclusionary master narratives, the top-down pressures placed on curriculum through high-stakes testing, and partisan rancor all combine to work against authentically supporting the civic mission of schools.

We argue that the state of democracy today in the United States is not, by default, evidence of the failure of education. Research points to successful curriculum pathways (Levine, 2003). Westheimer (2020) documented that curriculum allows for participatory or justice-oriented citizenship to develop if it: teaches students to ask questions, exposes students to multiple perspectives, teaches current controversial issues, focuses on the local, and is political. Lee et al. (2021) showed that gains would be substantial if all subject areas were to infuse their classrooms with dialogue and deliberation; after all, if classrooms are civic spaces, the opportunities and relationships established therein provide a form of civic education regardless of subject area. Shapiro and Brown (2018) acknowledged an underwhelming presence of comprehensive civic programs, but found that, when implemented, a three-dimensional model of civics is effective in strengthening students' civic capacities. Thus, the problem is not that civic education is not good enough; the problem is that the democratic ideals on which the United States was founded have yet to be realized. Educators today are not tasked with maintaining a democracy that provides equity and justice for all, we are being asked to create it.

Though the challenge looms large, we have a roadmap. The Equity in Civic Education Project (2020) engaged in a listening tour that carried team members across the United States to hear from schools and communities about how to improve civic education and opportunities. From conversations and observations taken during a moment of social upheaval—prompted by the developing Coronavirus pandemic and the racial reckoning following the murder of George Floyed—this team concluded:

> It is now time for us and the field to get to work in earnest. To advocate for both more *and* more equitable civic education everywhere—a type of civics that helps young people situate their own experiences in our imperfect but aspirational system of governance. A type of civics that helps students recognize the power they hold as a collective. A type of civics that does not shy away from hard content or difficult conversations and teaches the values of civic friendship, as well as the skills to combat bias and misinformation.
>
> (pp. 18–19)

For the field of art education, we see this call to action as an opportunity. As we have argued in Chapter 2 of this volume, 21st-century art education is predisposed to teach for civic agency. Furthermore, as we explored in Chapter 1, cultural citizenship offers an inclusive and powerful orientation that suggests how creative practices can take on a central role in supporting students' movement into becoming members of communities that matter to them. So, while traditional civics curriculum is beholden to covering a broad swath of civic knowledge, art education can address other areas by supporting civic values and skills.

As you move forward to develop your own curriculum, we ask you to consider what potential your community holds for inspiring civic values and skills. Art educators are needed to invent new ways for students and schools to engage in civic education. What can you and your students do to learn about your community's stories and unique contributions to the fabric of our nation? How might you bring this project to your whole school and do this learning in communion with others? How can you, the art teacher, offer up possibilities for engaging across subject matter in a civically engaged art curriculum that asks students to render themselves visible in the world?

References

Blake, W. O. (1860). *The history of slavery and the slave trade, ancient and modern. The forms of slavery that prevailed in ancient nations, particularly in Greece and Rome. The African slave trade and the political history of slavery in the United States.* H. Miller. https://library.si.edu/image-gallery/68463

Blandy, D. (2011). Sustainability, participatory culture, and the performance of democracy: Ascendant sites of theory and practice in art education. *Studies in Art Education, 52*(3), 243–255. https://doi.org/10.1080/00393541.2011.11518838

Childs, M. C. (2001). Civic ecosystems. *Journal of Urban Design, 6*(1), 55–72. https://doi.org/10.1080/13574800120032879

Duncombe, S. (2016). Does it work? The æffect of activist art. *Social Research, 83*(1), 115–134. https://doi.org/10.1353/sor.2016.0005

Hammer Projects: Kevin Beasley. (n.d.). Hammer. https://hammer.ucla.edu/exhibitions/2017/hammer-projects-kevin-beasley

Lee, C. D., White, G., & Dong, D. (2021). Educating for civic reasoning and discourse. National Academy of Education. https://naeducation.org/educating-for-civic-reasoning-and-discourse/

Levine, P. (2003). The civic mission of schools. *National Civic Review, 92*(4), 63–65. https://doi.org/10.1002/ncr.34

MacClure, M. (2010). The offence of theory. *Journal of Education Policy, 25*(2), 275–283. https://doi.org/10.1080/02680930903462316

MacClure, M. (2020). Inquiry as divination. *Qualitative Inquiry, 23*(4), 345–370. https://doi.org/10.1177/1077800420939124

Shapiro, S., & Brown, C. (2018). *The state of civics education.* Center for American Progress. https://www.americanprogress.org/issues/education-k-12/reports/2018/

Stefaniak, A., Bilewicz, M., & Lewicka, M. (2017). The merits of teaching local history: Increased place attachment enhances civic engagement and social trust. *Journal of Environmental Psychology, 51*, 217–225. https://doi.org/10.1016/j.jenvp.2017.03.014

Westheimer, J. (2020). Can education change the world? Kappa Delta Pi Record, 56(1), 6–12. https://doi.org/10.1080/00228958.2020.1696085

Willie Cole. (n.d.) MoMA. https://www.moma.org/collection/works/66215

Index

Note: **Bold** and *Italic* page numbers refer to tables and figures.

9781032057781